MUSSOLINI

From Socialist

D1425558

PERSONALITIES *and* POWERS

MUSSOLINI

From Socialist to Fascist

DAVID WILLIAMSON

Hodder & Stoughton

A MEMBER OF THE HODDER HEADLINE GROUP

For Mary, Antonia and Alex

Acknowledgements
The publishers would like to thank the following for their permission to
reproduce the following illustrations in this volume:
Hulton Getty, London, cover illustration; Camera Press, London, p. 15;
Estate of Kimon Marengo/Alex Marengo p. 77.

The publishers would like to thank the following for permission to
reproduce material in this volume:
Einaudi for extracts from *Mussolini il rivoluzionario* by R. De Felice
(1965), *Mussolini: il Duce, ii* by R. De Felice (1981), *L'organizzazione dello
stato totalitario* by A. Aquarome (1965) and ... *Voi siete la primavera* ...
l'ideolgia fascista nel monda della scuola, 1925–1943 by G. Biondi and F.
Imberciadori (1982); Fontana for an extract from *The Rome–Berlin Axis*
by E. Wiskemann (1966); Hutchinson and the Estate of Mussolini for
extracts from *My Autobiography*, by B. Mussolini (1928); Macmillan for
an extract from *Italian Fascism, 1919–1945* by P. Morgan (1995); Oxford
University Press for an extract from *Fascism in Ferrara* by P. Corner
(1975); Phoenix Paperback for an extract from *Mussolini* by D. Mack
Smith (1994); Routledge for an extract from *Italian Foreign Policy,
1870–1940* by C. J. Lowe and F. Mazari (1975); University of Michigan
Press for extracts from *Italy: a Modern History* by D. Mack Smith (1959).

Every effort has been made to trace and acknowledge ownership of
copyright. The publishers will be glad to make suitable arrangements
with any copyright holder whom it has not been possible to contact.

British Library Cataloguing in Publication Data
A catalogue for this title is available from the British Library

ISBN 0 340 658347

First published 1997
Impression number   10   9   8   7   6   5   4   3   2   1
Year   1999   1998   1997

Typeset by Fakenham Photosetting Limited, Fakenham, Norfolk.
Printed in Great Britain for Hodder & Stoughton Educational, a
division of Hodder Headline Plc, 338 Euston Road, London NW1 3BH
by Redwood Books, Trowbridge, Wiltshire.

CONTENTS

INTRODUCTION

Although Mussolini was later overshadowed by Hitler, he remains one of the key figures of the first half of the twentieth century. While the Nazi Party was still a small extremist party in Bavaria, Mussolini had by 1922 already turned the Fascist Party into a major political force in Italy. He cleverly used a widespread fear of the Communists, the desire of the middle classes for political change, the anger of the soldiers returning from the front with a government that could offer them no work, and the longing of the Nationalists for an Italian empire, to create a new party which seemed to offer a popular and novel alternative to socialism.

For 11 years Italy was the only Fascist state in Europe. Mussolini was seen by many contemporaries in Europe and America as a strong man who had replaced a chaotic democracy with a disciplined regime which, as some foreign visitors to Italy were to remark, at the very least made the trains run on time. Others, of course, saw him as little more than a thug, who destroyed free speech and set up a dictatorship. Mussolini's success was a major influence on Hitler. The way he took power by a mixture of constitutional legality and violence carried out by armed Fascist bands was to be copied by Hitler ten years later.

Mussolini established a dictatorship in Italy that lasted nearly 21 years. To some, Fascism seemed to have solved the problem of relations between employers and workers in a non-socialist way by establishing the corporative system in which both were equally represented. This image of harmony and discipline at home was strengthened by his successful foreign policy. In 1936 he carried out a long-standing Italian ambition when he conquered Ethiopia. Yet it was ultimately Mussolini's foreign policy that caused the collapse of Fascism. The fatal decision to ally with Germany and to declare war on Britain and France in June 1940 eventually led to his downfall. In 1943, when the Allies invaded Italy, his regime collapsed like a house of cards. It was only German intervention that kept alive a puppet Fascist state in the north. In April 1945 he was captured by anti-Fascist Italian forces and shot. His body was brought back to Milan where it was hung upside down in a petrol filling station.

His death, together with Hitler's, marked the end of the Fascist era. Since then the social conditions which gave rise to Fascism have disappeared, although right-wing successor parties have from time to time emerged. However, in Italy particularly, the Fascist period is still controversial and the causes and consequences of the rise of Fascism are bitterly debated.

MUSSOLINI THE SOCIALIST AND REBEL

CHILDHOOD AND SCHOOLING

Benito Mussolini was born on 29 July 1883 in a small, two-roomed cottage just outside the village of Predappio in the Romagna, in north-eastern Italy. It was a poor hilly area in which peasants had to struggle hard to make a living. Mussolini was particularly influenced by his father, who was a blacksmith and a revolutionary Socialist. His mother, on the other hand, was a devout Christian and a conscientious headmistress of the local school. He liked to claim later that he was born into the working classes, but this was not accurate. His family was not wealthy but it did own some land, could afford a servant and was able to keep Benito and his brother at school until they were 18.

Benito was a difficult child. He first went to a school run by monks where he reacted violently against the harsh discipline. Once, at the age of ten, he led a demonstration against the poor quality of the school's food. On another occasion he had to be dragged into the local church to attend Mass, which was compulsory for the whole school. He rapidly became a gang leader and was finally expelled for stabbing another boy at supper. At his next school he was suspended three times for fighting and bullying, but his potential ability as a public speaker was recognised when he was asked to deliver a speech to an audience in the town's theatre commemorating the famous Italian composer, Verdi.

In 1901 he qualified as a teacher. He already had a reputation as a Socialist, an eccentric intellectual and a successful seducer of women. He composed poetry and read widely. He managed to find a temporary post in the local village school at Gualtieri, where he also acted as secretary of a small Socialist group and wrote for some left-wing magazines, but Mussolini's lifestyle, which involved drinking, gambling and an affair with a married woman, ensured that his contract was not renewed in 1902.

THE ITALY OF MUSSOLINI'S YOUTH

In 1900 Italy was a comparatively new state which had been fully unified for only 30 years. The unification left a legacy of problems that were still not fully overcome by 1914 and which helped prepare the way for Mussolini's success in 1922. At first only about half a million Italians had the vote and the government of Italy was carried out by coalitions of a tightly-knit group of politicians, most of whom came from the upper middle classes of northern Italy. Many of these were convinced that Italy was destined to become a great power and to build up an empire in North Africa, although Italy quite clearly lacked the economic resources to be a major imperial power. Italy successfully annexed Eritrea and a part of Somaliland, but all further expansion came abruptly to a halt when the Ethiopians destroyed an Italian army at Adowa in 1896.

In the 1880s Italy was still mainly agricultural and much of the population was poor and illiterate. In many parts of the country, particularly the south, there was no feeling of national consciousness. There the peasants were preoccupied with the struggle to survive and viewed the government almost as a foreign power. This feeling of alienation was reinforced by the Papacy's refusal to recognise the new Italian state, which had absorbed its territories during the struggle for unification (see Chaper 5).

However by the 1890s Italy began to change. In the north around Milan, Turin and Genoa rapid industrialisation took place. This in turn created an urban working class and at the same time the schools in the expanding cities helped produce a new 'lower middle class' which was ambitious to fill the technical and managerial jobs being created by industrialisation. Quite quickly this began to alter the pattern of Italian politics. The electoral reform of 1881, which had increased the electorate to two million, enabled new parties to be set up. In 1892 the Italian Socialist Party was founded, as well as Republican and Catholic parties. The 1890s also witnessed a series of bitter strikes and riots, which impressed the young Mussolini and turned him into a Socialist. The reaction of the more conservative-minded politicians to these events was to try to ban the Socialist Party and the trade unions. Although they failed, this hostility to democracy provides a clue as to why the Right in Italian politics after the First World War proved so ready to support the Fascist Party.

Between 1900 and early 1914, the Liberal politician Giovanni Giolitti made a determined effort to create a new base of support built around the southern landowners, the industrialists in the north, the rural Catholic clergy and the moderate Socialists. If he had succeeded the Constitutional state would have been much stronger in 1922 and Mussolini might well not have been able to come to power. However three factors prevented Giolitti's success: the economic depression of 1907–8, the hostile reaction from the workers to the annexation of Libya in 1912, and the introduction of universal manhood suffrage that same year. These factors all helped push Italian socialism further to the left, which in turn provoked a violent reaction from the Right. The new Nationalist movement under Alfredo Rocco and Enrico Corradini, for instance, agitated for a strong political leadership that would unite the nation and expand the empire. In March 1914 Giolitti was defeated and a new right–centre government was formed by Antonio Salandra with the intention of creating an anti-Socialist middle-class bloc to govern Italy.

MUSSOLINI IN SWITZERLAND, 1902–4

In June 1902 Mussolini fled to Switzerland. He wanted to escape both military service, with which as a Socialist he violently disagreed, having to pay his debts, and the consequences of several embarrassing love affairs. For a short time he lived in doss houses or else slept under the Grand Pont, the bridge in Lausanne where homeless people gathered at night to sleep. He held a number of temporary jobs and again became involved in left-wing politics when he became the secretary of a builders' union, the members of which were mainly Italian immigrants. At one stage he was arrested as an agitator and handed over to the Italian police, but managed to get back to Switzerland with a forged passport. He also tried to encourage fellow Italians to desert from the army. When later he was in power, Mussolini tried, of course, to keep any record of this secret. Instead stories were told about him as a scholar and philosopher, who attended Geneva and Zurich universities. He actually did attend a few lectures at Lausanne and undoubtedly read widely, all of which was to help him later when he became a journalist. In 1904 when the Italian government promised not to punish deserters, Mussolini decided after all to return and complete his military service.

TEACHER AND JOURNALIST

Mussolini completed his military service without incident. Indeed in an effort to impress his superior officers he even privately wrote to one of them telling him how patriotic he was. This letter, which went completely against his principles, is an early example of how he was ready to compromise himself in order to achieve success. He left the Army in 1906 and took up another teaching post in a village in the mountainous area near the Austrian frontier. He was a poor teacher, who could only keep his pupils quiet by bribing them with sweets, and whose lifestyle again scandalised his headmaster. In 1908 he at last found a job which he enjoyed and was good at when he became part-time editor of the small Socialist periodical *La Lima*. In that year he also had a chance to try out his talents as a political agitator when the farm workers in his home village of Predappio went on strike. Under his leadership they attacked the new threshing machines and troops had to be called in to keep order. Mussolini was even arrested and taken to the local town escorted by a squadron of cavalry.

Early in 1909 he moved over the border to the Italian-speaking province of Trentino in the Austrian Empire and, after editing a Socialist weekly for six months, became the sub-editor of a fiercely patriotic and anti-Austrian paper. It is possible that this started the process that would gradually turn Mussolini into a super patriot and Fascist, although at this stage he annoyed many Nationalists by arguing that the workers were quite correctly not interested in patriotism. It also taught him a lot about popular journalism and, as Mack Smith put it, 'how to write a whole article about some non-event without arousing disbelief'.

MUSSOLINI'S IDEAS

How genuine was Mussolini's socialism? Many contemporaries came to the conclusion that he had no fixed set of beliefs. Angelica Balabanoff, a Russian Socialist whom he got to know in Lausanne, believed that it was:

> more the reflection of his early environment and his own rebellious egoism than the products of understanding and conviction . . . it sprang rather from his own sense of indignity and frustration, from a passion to assert his own ego and from a determination for personal revenge.

Yet it would be inaccurate simply to argue that Mussolini's socialism had no intellectual base. He was certainly influenced by the revolutionary syndicalists, A. O. Olivetti and S. Panunzio. Although he rejected their faith in trade unions as a revolutionary weapon, he approved of their belief in direct action and violence in politics. Mussolini was, too, much impressed by the new theories of crowd psychology and the importance of élite groups in history, which Vilfredo Pareto, Gaetano Mosca and Gustave Le Bon were writing about. He was also influenced by the German philosopher, Nietzsche, and admired his hatred and scorn for the Christian virtues of humility and kindness. He was particularly impressed by Nietzsche's characterisation of the imaginary figure of the 'Superman', who trampled ruthlessly on the weak. The German historian Ernst Nolte describes Mussolini as a Marxist during this period. It is of course true that Mussolini was no intellectual theorist like Lenin, but at this stage he did nevertheless have much in common with him. He believed in the class struggle and the eventual revolution of the workers and peasants. Like the Marxists, he also believed that the workers of the world should unite. When Italy invaded Libya in 1911, he argued fiercely that Socialists should not be patriotic and loyal to Italy. This often contradictory mixture of ideas shows that Mussolini was no orthodox Socialist and that at some point he might become a rallying point for many outside the main stream of socialism. He had no real sympathy with the workers and peasants. He urged revolution and the abolition of private property, not out of a desire to help them but rather to smash the existing political structure and replace it by a small dynamic dictatorship of the workers.

THE SOCIALIST AGITATOR AND POLITICIAN

In 1910 Mussolini left Austria. He married Rachele Guidi, the daughter of his father's mistress, and settled down in the small town of Forli where he took up a new job as political organiser of the local Socialist clubs. He also became the editor of a small weekly publication called *The Class Struggle*. He rapidly emerged as an ambitious politician. In October, at the Socialist Party Congress, he bitterly criticised his party for not being revolutionary enough and in the following year, like Lenin, he actually broke away from the Party and tried to form a rival Socialist group. He got very little backing, but he was saved from the consequences of this impulsive act by the government's decision to occupy Libya. The Socialist movement united in opposition against this policy, and Mussolini played a key role in the anti-war protest. He organised a series of violent riots in Forli, which he hoped would escalate into a revolution. His reputation as an anti-imperialist was greatly increased when he was arrested and imprisoned. On his release he rejoined the Socialists and was actually voted on to the Party's directorate. A few months later Mussolini, as an ambitious politician, was given the marvellous opportunity of becoming the editor of the leading Socialist daily paper, *Avanti!* He was now in a position to influence both his party and national opinion. He strongly supported the peasants' cause when a wave of rural unrest swept Italy in 1913. Some ten years later he was to hush up this period of his career and pretend that he was already a Nationalist and trying to create a strong self-confident Italy. In fact Mussolini was highly critical of the moderate Socialist parties in Europe which voted for increases in the military budgets for their countries' armed forces. In words that contradicted everything he stood for later he urged:

> Let us have no more talk of battleships, barracks, cannon, at a time when thousands of villages have no schools, roads, electricity or doctors but still live tragically beyond the pale of civilized life.

However, he was of course no pacifist. If a war was to break out he believed that the workers and soldiers should rise up against the government. At one stage he was actually calling for the 'physical extermination' of the upper middle classes (bourgeoisie). By 1914 it was already clear that Mussolini undoubtedly had the potential to be a major political figure. He was a brilliant journalist who knew how to manipulate and impress public opinion. He was, too, a ruthless, charismatic figure who appealed to the younger Italian Socialists impatiently demanding radical policies from the Party leadership.

timeline	1883	29 July	Birth of Mussolini
	1901		First teaching post
	1902–4		'Exile' in Switzerland
	1909		Secretary to Chamber of Labour and editor of weekly Socialist paper in Trentino
	1910		Mussolini marries
	1910–12		Editor of *The Class Struggle*
	1911		The Libyan War
	1912–14		Editor of *Avanti!*

Points to consider

1) **How much of a Socialist was Mussolini before 1914?**
2) **What qualities as a leader and organiser did Mussolini show before 1914?**

'ONLY BLOOD MAKES THE WHEELS OF HISTORY TURN' – MUSSOLINI AND THE FIRST WORLD WAR

When the First World War started in August 1914, Mussolini at first, like all his fellow Socialists, argued that Italy should stay out of the war, yet by the autumn he began to change his mind. In some ways he was merely swinging back to what he had always believed. He was becoming convinced that this war might cause the very revolution he longed for and which would create a Socialist Italy. Thus on 18 October 1914 he surprised his party by suddenly suggesting in *Avanti!* that Italy should ally with Britain and France. He was, however, unable to win the Party around and was forced to resign.

THE PRO-WAR AGITATOR

Mussolini's expulsion from the Party was one of the most important turning points in his career. Although at the time he denied it, it marked effectively the end of his period as a Socialist. To survive he needed to make contacts with the Nationalists and industrialists, who were the very people whom he had attacked so bitterly in *Avanti!* He immediately started a new pro-war paper, *Il Popolo d'Italia*, which received subsidies not only from Britain and France but also the Italian industrialists, who reckoned that war would increase their profits. Even if he had wanted to, he had little choice but to sound a more nationalistic note in the editorials in his paper. He started to talk about 'the immense booty' that Italy could win in the Balkans and the Middle East and he even came round to arguing that the Libyan War of 1911–12 had been fully justified!

Like most of the interventionists, he joined one of the small revolutionary action groups called *fasci di azione rivoluzionaria* that were springing up to agitate for Italian intervention on the side of the Allies in the war. The pro-war movement anticipated the later post-war Fascist movement in that it combined both right-wing and left-wing elements in a revolt against the old Liberal politicians. In his autobiography Mussolini described how

> Standing by me and helping my work as a newspaperman were the *Fascisti* [members of the *fasci*]. They were composed of revolutionary spirits who believed in intervention. They were youths – the students of the universities, the Socialist syndicalists [those who believe that industries should be controlled by the workers themselves], destroying faith in Karl Marx by their ideals. There were professional men, too, who could still hear the real voice of the Country!
>
> (Benito Mussolini, *My Autobiography*, Hutchinson, 1928, p. 49)

Mussolini claimed that he had created the *Fascisti* in December 1914 but it is more accurate to say that he first joined the *Fascisti* and then took them over in December. They were only a small and relatively insignificant group at that time, but they did enable him to back up his words with a show of force. Pressure was also exerted on the government by large demonstrations organised by the Nationalists and the action groups. Mussolini, for instance, managed to bring together a crowd of 30 000 people in Milan. Later he was to call this the start of the Fascist revolution, but in reality the members of the *fasci* were very much the junior partners of the Nationalists and in any case some historians argue that the effect of this violence on the government was exaggerated.

---

a note on . . .

---

a) ITALY'S ENTRY INTO THE WAR

Italy was officially an ally of Germany, with whom she had concluded an alliance in 1882, but she remained neutral when war broke out. This was supported by a majority in parliament, but opposed by a mixed bunch of revolutionary Syndicalists, Conservatives and Nationalists, left-wing Liberals and Republicans. The latter two parties wanted to associate Italy with the two western democracies of Britain and France, whom they saw as 'the forces of progress'. The Syndicalists, like Mussolini, hoped that war might lead to revolution, while the Nationalists hoped for territorial gains at the expense of Austria and Turkey. Salandra, the Conservative Prime Minister, also believed that war would unite the Italian people. In April 1915, tempted by the terms offered by the Allies, the government secretly negotiated the Treaty of London with Britain and France: Italy would go to war against Austria in return for territorial gains at the end of the war. A month later without any proper debate in parliament the government declared war on Austria. The opposition, not only frightened by widespread pro-war rioting, also realised that the Treaty of London could not be dishonoured without causing a major constitutional crisis, which might lead to the resignation of the King, and the isolation of Italy in Europe.

b) THE ORIGINS OF THE WORD 'FASCIST'

Small groups of *Fascisti* – or members of a *fascio* (plural *fasci*) – were formed soon after the outbreak of war. They were left-wing interventionists, most of whom had left the Socialist Party just before Mussolini was expelled. In Italian the word *fascio* means bundle or, in this context, a small group of people. Later Mussolini stressed its link with ancient Rome: in Latin *fasces* were bundles of rods from the middle of which an axe stuck out, symbolising Roman justice.

MUSSOLINI AS A SOLDIER

Mussolini was called up in September 1915 and fought for two years in the trenches. He was certainly a competent and reasonably brave soldier who, like millions of other men all over Europe, endured the dangers and extreme discomforts of trench warfare. Later, of course, he was to claim that his war record was one of exemplary bravery, but there is little evidence of this. In 1917 he was wounded on a training exercise when a grenade thrower blew up. His wounds were not serious, although they did cause him to be invalided out of the army. Later, in an extraordinary expression which shows how he came to glorify war, he described the incident as 'the most beautiful moment in my life'.

IMPACT OF THE WAR ON ITALY

Salandra assumed that the war would be brief and victorious, but it dragged on until November 1918, and did create the potentially revolutionary situation which Mussolini longed for. The old ruling class was deeply divided in its attitude to the war and in effect paralysed. In October 1917 the Italians suffered a disastrous defeat at Caporetto at the hands of the Austrians (with some German support), and in order to carry the people with them the government launched a major propaganda campaign. The peasants' expectations were raised by the promise of land reform and, similarly, the middle classes' by changes in the political system which would give them more influence. The government's great hope, of course, was that territorial gains in the Balkans, North Africa and the Middle East would in the end make the war worth fighting, but the entry of the United States, which was opposed to the annexation of Balkan territory, into the war in April 1917 and the rise of nationalism in the Balkans indicated that these objectives would not be easy to secure. Inevitably failure here would mean bitter disappointment for the Nationalists. The Bolshevik revolution also had a profound impact on the Italian workers and provided a model which the left wing of the Socialist Party could try to use in Italy.

RETURN TO JOURNALISM

Back in civilian life in 1917 Mussolini took up the editorship of *Il Popolo d'Italia* again and poured out a stream of articles commenting on the growing national crisis. Increasingly in its pages he argued that only a dictatorship could secure victory for Italy and he even discussed with the Commander-in-Chief of the Italian Army the possibility of setting one up. Mussolini also began to draw up a possible agenda for a new post-war party, which could appeal to the returning soldiers. He sketched out a programme which would help the poor by giving industrial workers a share in their company's profits, reducing their working day to eight hours and giving the landless peasants smallholdings. At the same time he appealed to the Nationalists by demanding the annexation of Trieste, Fiume and most of Dalmatia. He dismissed Marxism as a 'heap of ruins' and even began cautiously to support capitalism. He countered the criticisms of his former Socialist comrades by arguing that 'every intelligent man must change his views'. As an ambitious politician who had cut himself off from the Socialists he was anxious to create a new party which would be able to win mass support in post-war Italy. He realised that whatever happened he must somehow remain a controversial figure and produce a programme that would appeal to a wide range of voters. He did not hesitate to steal ideas from other parties. Already by December 1918 he was more interested in power than ideals and theories. He began to sense that he could exploit the post-war mood of disillusionment in Italy. In his biography he wrote somewhat grandly:

> The lovely structure of concord and harmony that we combatants and the wounded had dreamed that we would build after the luminous victory of 1918 was coming to pieces . . . I sensed the chills and heats of decay and destruction.
>
> (*My Autobiography*, pp. 65–6)

timeline	1914	October	Mussolini resigns from *Avanti!*
		November	Sets up *Il Popolo d'Italia*
	1915	May	Italy declares war on Austria
		September	Mussolini joins the Army
	1917	February	Is wounded on training exercise
		June	He again takes over the editorship of *Il Popolo*
	1918	November	Hostilities end – armistices signed between Austria and Italy and Germany and the Allies

Points to consider

1) Why did Mussolini resign from the editorship of the *Avanti!*?
2) Why did he begin to become a Nationalist?
3) How did he plan to exploit the post-war situation in Italy?
4) How did the war affect Italian politics?

THE CREATION OF THE FASCIST PARTY AND THE SEIZURE OF POWER

POST-WAR PROBLEMS

After the war Italy, like all the other European countries, was faced with severe economic and social problems. Supplies of food and raw materials were scarce, inflation was high and threatened the savings and security of the middle classes. There was little work for the demobilised soldiers returning from the trenches and parts of the countryside were terrorised by bands of deserters who plundered the local farmers. The years 1918–20 were called the *biennio rosso,* or the red years, as there were widespread strikes and unrest in both the towns and the countryside. Trade union membership increased and the numbers joining the Socialist Party reached an all time high. With the frightening example of the Russian revolution very much in their minds the Italian middle classes, industrialists and landowners were convinced that Italy was on the brink of revolution. Looking back it is clear that this fear was exaggerated, but the militancy of some of the Socialists created an atmosphere of fear and hatred amongst many Italians. For instance in 1919 in many Italian cities anything symbolising the war or the propertied classes attracted violence. Not only were officers and private citizens wearing ties or hats in danger of being beaten up but sometimes even wounded war veterans had their crutches kicked away from them. Not surprisingly millions of Italians began to wish for a strong government that would make Italy both safe and prosperous.

The government was criticised for its failure to maintain internal order and rebuild the economy, and was also bitterly attacked by the

Nationalists when it failed in the Paris peace negotiations to gain Dalmatia and an extensive empire in the Middle East and North Africa. In September 1919 the predominantly Italian-speaking city of Fiume in the Adriatic was declared a 'free' or self-governing city by the Treaty of St Germain, instead of being handed over to Italy. In protest it was occupied by a gang of Italian ex-soldiers led by the flamboyant Nationalist Gabriele D'Annunzio. It was not until December 1920 that the government was able to expel him.

For an ambitious politician like Mussolini it soon became clear that there was potentially a lot of support to be gained by projecting himself as the strong man who could restore order at home and simultaneously make Italy great abroad where the weak Liberal politicians had so miserably failed. The lesson from D'Annunzio's daring coup in Fiume was also not lost on Mussolini. Direct action or a 'march on Rome' might succeed better than constitutional politics and the ballot box.

---

a note on . . .

ITALIAN POLITICS 1919–22

After the war proportional representation was introduced as a system of voting in Italian general elections. It was more democratic than the old system as it allotted parliamentary seats to the parties according to the percentage of votes they won. In the elections of 1919 two major parties emerged: the *Popolari* and the Socialists with 100 and 156 seats respectively. The Popolari was in some ways a left-wing party. It condemned imperialism and wanted the large rural estates divided up amongst the peasantry, but it also contained many conservative Catholics. Don Sturzo, its leader, therefore hesitated to cooperate with the Socialists for fear of splitting the Party. If the Socialists and Popolari had cooperated, they would have provided Italy with a stable government and so blocked the rise of Fascism. Instead hostility between them ensured that a series of weak and unstable coalitions headed by pre-war Liberal politicians formed short-lived governments. The Liberals who had been bitterly divided into 'interventionists' and 'neutralists' during the war were still deeply split. Between June 1919 and October 1922, when Mussolini came to power, there were four different prime ministers: Nitti, Giolitti, Bonomi and Facta.

Mussolini in a more relaxed moment

THE FASCIST MOVEMENT

Mussolini founded the Fascist movement in Milan on 23 March 1919 at a meeting in an obscure hall attended by some 50 people. The founder members had little in common as they were a diverse collection of Catholics, Nationalists, Liberals and Anarchists. Mussolini, through whose paper the meeting had been announced, sketched out in a speech a radical programme which essentially became the official manifesto of the movement in June. Potentially the movement was offering the Italians something radically new. In his autobiography Mussolini talked of Fascism as being an 'anti-party':

> It was not to be tied to old or new schools of any kind. . . . I felt that it was not only the anti-Socialist battle we had to fight; this was only a battle on the way. There was a lot more to do . . . In a word . . . it was necessary to lay the foundation of a new civilisation.
>
> (*My Autobiography*, p. 73)

What form this new civilisation was to take could be seen from the programme which announced to the Italian people:

> Here is the national programme of a solidly Italian movement. Revolutionary, because it is opposed to dogma and demogogy; robustly innovating because it rejects preconceived opinions. We prize above everything else the experience of a revolutionary war.
>
> (Quoted in R. De Felice, *Mussolini il rivoluzionario*, Einaudi, 1965, pp. 744–5

The programme went on to demand universal suffrage, constitutional reform, the creation of national technical councils to be elected by professional or trade organisations, an eight-hour day, a minimum wage and social insurance legislation. There was also to be a heavy tax on capital and confiscation of excessive war profits. Finally, a national militia or people's army was to be set up. Essentially, as Mussolini made clear in his speech on 23 March these reforms were to help those who 'were returning from the trenches'.

What was new about the Fascist movement was that it was aimed at the new class created by the war – the 3.5 million men who were called up to fight. It was above all a movement rather than a party, which could attract a very diverse membership. *Fasci*, or branches were established in Bologna, Padua and Florence, but in Italy as a whole it received relatively little attention. It recruited, for the most part, ex-servicemen like the *Arditi*, who had been specially trained assault troops in the war; also intellectuals, who were members of the Futurist cultural movement which had the curious aim of enthusing artists with a love of war and modern industry. A small number of patriotic Socialists joined who, like Mussolini himself, had broken with the official Socialist Party. The *Arditi* were particularly useful allies as they provided Mussolini with the nucleus of the Fascist squads which were later to enable him to terrorise the streets and to cow the Socialists. As early as April 1919, for example, the *Arditi* smashed up the offices of the Socialist paper *Avanti!*

THE ELECTORAL FAILURE OF 1919

Since the election of 1919 was the first to be fought under the new system of proportional representation, Mussolini optimistically hoped that the Fascists would make some gains, but they failed to win a single seat. This was largely because they were badly organised and had no common programme. Mussolini campaigned in Milan on a left-wing programme, but elsewhere the local Fascists themselves decided what line to take.

Mussolini's first reaction to this failure was to think about emigrating, but when he was able to make a calmer assessment of the situation he soon realised that Fascism was very far from a spent force. Nitti was unable to win backing for his government in parliament. The more conservative Liberals thought Nitti too friendly to the workers, while the *Popolari* and the Socialists did not believe that his proposed reforms went far enough. The large Socialist Party sitting in parliament frightened the right-wing parties and the industrialists, and led them to look upon the *Arditi* as a possible counter-revolutionary force that could smash the Socialists. Above all, in the pages of *Il Popolo d'Italia*, the newpaper which he both edited and controlled, he had a very effective means of getting his message across to important sections of the Italian people.

THE RESURGENCE OF FASCISM

After the electoral disasters of November 1919 membership of the initial Fascist movement sank to a mere 870 members, yet by the end of 1920 it had risen to 250000 members. This spectacular increase was the result of a two-pronged movement: one based on the towns and led by Mussolini, and the other a spontaneous rural movement which was a reaction to the agricultural strikes organised by the peasant leagues. By December 1921 there was a whole network of Fascist organisations in the major cities and countryside of northern and central Italy. Mussolini's own power base was in Milan. The other *fasci* were virtually independent of him and under their own *ras*, or chiefs, as they were called in imitation of the local chieftains in Ethiopia. *Ras*, like Italo Balbo of Ferrara, a former student and ex-officer, and Roberto Farinacci in Cremona, a railway official, were powerful and independent barons in their own right. They attracted a radical membership which consisted of students, young professionals, like teachers, architects and lawyers, many of whom had been junior officers in the war, and small shopkeepers. While the *fasci* were anti-Socialist and thus attracted the financial backing of industrialists and landowners, they were a revolutionary force in their own right. They wanted to reshape and modernise Italian politics so that the middle classes themselves held the power.

The *fasci* in the cities organised combat squads which went out into the surrounding countryside and destroyed the local headquarters of the peasant leagues and of the Socialist Party, whose leaders were seized and given often lethal beatings and forced to drink large doses of castor oil. In the countryside new *fasci* were set up which won the backing of the middle and upper-middle classes, landowners, the more prosperous peasantry, tenant farmers, and estate managers, who were all opposed to rural socialism which aimed to collectivise or take over the land from private ownership. It soon became clear that the Fascists were not just puppets of the great landowners. They had their own plans for organising the peasants into Fascist labour unions and settling the landless peasants on land owned by the local *fascio* or donated by the gentry. At this stage then Fascism was far from being a unified movement. It was much more a complex network of local groups which were linked together by patriotism and anti-socialism and eventually the acceptance of Mussolini as *Duce* – or leader.

MUSSOLINI THE OPPORTUNIST

In the course of 1920 Mussolini began to appreciate that his best chance of political success was to appeal to the anti-socialism of the Nationalists and the Conservatives, but he was still careful not to identify too strongly with the Right. He insisted that there was a place in the Fascist movement for people with every shade of political belief, and through *Il Popolo d'Italia* he was able to articulate the demands of both the urban and rural Fascists and keep himself prominently in the public eye. His overriding ambition was to gain power. Under certain circumstances he could still have been tempted to lead a workers' revolt. When, for example, several factories in northern Italy were occupied by workers in the autumn of 1920, Mussolini met their leaders secretly and apparently hinted that he could be the man they needed, but he rapidly abandoned that idea when the strikes collapsed. Instead he returned to the potentially powerful idea of nationalism and championed Italy's claims to Dalmatia and Albania. His main rival on the Right was D'Annunzio, whose coup in Fiume seemed at one point to be a prelude to the creation of a new authoritarian regime for the whole of Italy. D'Annunzio initially regarded Mussolini as his chief propagandist and fund raiser, but the latter skilfully distanced himself from his charismatic rival and realised that the way to power did not lie through the distant outpost of Fiume but rather through exploiting the widespread fear of socialism and communism in Italy. Thus he secretly welcomed the government's decision to eject D'Annunzio from Fiume in December 1920 as it effectively destroyed the power base of his main rival.

MUSSOLINI ENTERS PARLIAMENT

In May 1921 Giolitti in an attempt to win a majority for the governing coalition called another general election. As the left wing of the Socialists had broken away to form the Communist Party, there was a real possibility that the remaining more moderate Socialists might be tempted to ally with Giolitti. If this had happened, Italian politics would have been more stable and Mussolini effectively excluded from power. To prevent this Mussolini managed to convince Giolitti that he rather than the Socialists would be the more valuable ally. Giolitti made the same mistake as the German Conservatives were to make ten years later with Hitler – he believed that he would be able to tame Mussolini, while using the Fascists, particularly the thugs on the streets, to weaken his opponents. Not surprisingly the election was extremely violent and about 100 people were killed. The Fascist attacks on the Socialists and

Communists were openly tolerated by both the police and the army, who even lent them weapons and transport, yet despite all this Mussolini won only 35 seats in parliament, while the Socialists and *Popolari* won 122 and 107 seats respectively.

Not only had Giolitti decisively failed to strengthen his position, but once parliament met Mussolini deserted him and pursued an independent line, which seemed to be full of contradictions. At one stage he proposed a coalition between the Fascists and the *Popolari*, perhaps in the hope that this would enable him to form a government or at least persuade the Conservatives to make a rival bid for his cooperation. In August 1921 he then signed a 'pact of pacification' with the Socialists. Did this mean that he was suddenly reverting to his former left-wing policies? In fact it was part of a strategy to strengthen his grip on Fascism. If Fascism was to become an effective political force, it had to be less of a dynamic movement and more of an organised political party under Mussolini's own control. Mussolini was concerned about the political implications of the reign of terror that the *ras* had let loose on the northern and central Italian countryside. While in principle not opposing this violence, as it was doing much to destroy the power bases of the Socialists, Mussolini nevertheless believed that it might go too far and force the government to intervene with troops to restore order. Once that happened he feared that the whole Fascist movement might be outlawed and destroyed. In October he at last managed to create an organised National Fascist Party (PNF), which set up local branches, regularly collected subscriptions and attracted respectable middle-class members. The new party was a counterweight to the squads and enabled Mussolini to bargain with the politicians in Rome.

The Rome congress

When the *ras* refused to accept the pacification pact with the Socialists, Mussolini took the considerable risk of resigning his position as leader (*Duce*) of the Fascist Movement. He gambled that his charisma and oratory would soon see him reinstalled. In this he was correct. In November at the third Fascist national congress in Rome he explained his policies, and even conceded that he had been mistaken to negotiate with the Socialists, in a brilliant speech that won him back his position as *Duce*. The speech was a triumph. The congress agreed that the control of the movement should be centralised under Mussolini, but significantly the *ras* were allowed to keep their squads of blackshirts and continue with a policy of violence.

THE GOVERNMENT OF LUIGI FACTA

In the political crisis caused by the fall in January 1922 of Bonomi's government, which had only been in power for six months, the Fascist squads were to be a key element in Mussolini's seizure of power. There was no clear successor government and King Victor Emmanuel interviewed each party leader in turn, including Mussolini, in the hope that one of them might be able to form a cabinet. Eventually, after nearly a month, a weak minority government was formed under Luigi Facta, whom one historian has called 'a timid ignorant provincial lawyer who had risen in politics by seniority alone'. This government proved to be only a stop-gap and it collapsed in July. Once again none of the other parties' leaders was ready to risk forming a government and Facta returned to power in August.

THE TRIUMPH OF VIOLENCE

The prolonged political crisis in Rome and the emergence of the weak Facta cabinet created an ideal situation for Mussolini. There was little prospect of any firm action being taken against the Fascist squads and at the same time he could claim that they were simply protecting the state from a Communist revolution. In February 1922 when a Fascist was killed in Fiume, his comrades seized a destroyer in the port and overthrew the elected town council. When the government ignored this, Mussolini felt safe enough to launch attacks on Socialist-run cities elsewhere in Italy. Milan, Ferrara, Cremona, Leghorn, Parma and Ravenna, for example, all had their elected city councils forcibly pushed out of power. In August the Socialists played right into his hands when they made the mistake of calling a general strike as a protest against the government's inability to keep order. Mussolini immediately announced that if the government would not act against the strikers, his squads would have to. He could thus both pose as the protector of order and at the same time destroy the printing presses and headquarters of his enemies, the Socialists. These measures were highly effective and ensured that when Mussolini became Prime Minister in October the Socialists were not prepared to stop him.

By the early autumn of 1922 Mussolini had no rivals on the Right. D'Annunzio had lost his power base in Fiume and forfeited his chance of winning over the *ras* by criticising the activities of the squads in the countryside, and the *ras* themselves were too compromised by violence to be able to lead the Fascist Party in parliament. The way was therefore open for him to pursue a dual track strategy of 'conciliation and threat' (P. Morgan). He was perceived by the Conservatives and many Liberals to be the only man who could control the excesses of the *ras*. Consequently he was able to blackmail the King and the politicians into agreeing to his appointment as Prime Minister. He cleverly pursued a policy which gave out contradictory messages to the Italian public. On the one hand he hinted that if he became Prime Minister, he would act as a normal constitutional politician would, concerned with balancing the budget and making the existing system work, and like any good Nationalist politician, aim to make Italy the most important power in the Mediterranean. On the other hand he allowed the *ras* to step up the violence and even attack non-Socialist town councils like those of Bolzano and Trent. It was a highly effective technique which enabled him with considerable political skill to manoeuvre himself into power.

Middle-class public opinion was ready to tolerate Mussolini not because they liked him but because they thought that he would restore some discipline to Italy, save it from the Communists and create a new regime in which they would have much more power. In an environment where public services like the post and the railways were deteriorating alarmingly and the crime rate was shooting up there seemed to be something to be said for a strong man in power. In the towns which they controlled the Fascists enforced the law in a crude but effective way. For instance in Adria, a town south of Venice, they eliminated alcoholism by threatening to make anybody who was caught drunk consume a pint of castor oil!

The seizure of power

Mussolini was careful to keep every option open while he was planning to seize power. His task was made easier by the divisions amongst the leading Liberal politicians, who all thought that they could use Mussolini to strengthen their own position and defeat their political rivals. Mussolini cleverly played on this rivalry by telling each politician secretly that he wanted him to head a new coalition with the Fascists. Thus not surprisingly Giolitti, Facta, Nitti and Salandra were all pressing for some sort of governing coalition with him. Mussolini also tried to reassure both the King and the Pope that he was basically a safe man to have in power. However, he did not rule out using force. He was only too aware that if his negotiations with the politicians failed, he would have to risk an armed uprising. Otherwise Fascism might just collapse or be taken over by one of the *ras*, like Balbo, for instance. Thus on 16 October 1922 Mussolini and the Fascist leaders agreed on a plan for an armed uprising, although privately he continued to tell the politicians that he wanted to work with them within a parliamentary coalition. Yet the longer Mussolini delayed the greater was the danger that the *ras* would act independently of him. Thus on 24 October, in an effort to reassure the Party militants, he told a large meeting of Fascists from southern Italy that:

> either we are allowed to govern, or we will seize power by marching on Rome [to] take by the throat the miserable political class that governs us.
>
> (Quoted in D. Mack Smith, *Mussolini*, Phoenix Paperback, 1994, p. 51)

The uprising began during the night of 27–28 October when armed Fascists began to seize government offices all over Italy. Facta at last acted decisively and asked the King to declare an act of emergency which would allow him to order the army to intervene. It is most likely that this would have been successful and have led to the decisive defeat of Fascism. By 6 am in the morning of 28 October the army, in anticipation of the emergency decree, had already restored order in Milan. However some three hours later the King then changed his mind and refused to sign the decree. Why did he do this? Probably like many of his subjects he had little trust in Facta's ability to control the mounting violence in Italy. Facta's rival, Salandra, quite specifically advised the King not to sign because he hoped that this would lead to the former's resignation and a new government headed by himself. The King was also quite wrongly advised that the army would not be able to defend Rome from the Fascists. Like so many of the politicians, he optimistically believed that Mussolini could be absorbed into a coalition and tamed. Facta resigned in protest against his refusal to sign the decree. The King thereupon invited Salandra to form the next government. Mussolini was asked to join this, but refused believing that the monarch would eventually have to appoint him as Prime Minister. This analysis proved to be correct. Salandra was unable to form a government and advised Victor Emmanuel to appoint Mussolini, which he did on 29 October.

Mussolini had won power constitutionally, although, of course the threat of violence was always in the background. For propaganda purposes he was now anxious to give the impression that he had seized power only after some 300 000 armed Fascists had marched on Rome. In fact this was a myth. Mussolini went to Rome in a railway sleeping car, while a mere 25 000 disorganised and poorly armed Fascists reached Rome the next day. Again had there been the political will, the army could easily have dispersed them. 'The "march on Rome"', as Denis Mack Smith has written, 'was thus a comfortable train ride, followed by a petty demonstration, and all in response to an express invitation from the monarch.'

timeline	1919	March	Formation of first Fascist Combat group
		September	D'Annunzio's raid on Fiume
		November	General Election – Fascists gain no seats
	1920	June	Giovanni Giolitti replaces Nitti
		September	Workers occupy factories in N. Italy
	1921	January	Italian Communist Party formed
		May	General Election – Fascists gain 35 seats
		July	Ivan Bonomi replaces Giolitti
		August	The Fascist–Socialist 'pact of pacification'
		November	The Third National Congress of Fascism
	1922	February	Luigi Facta replaces Bonomi
		August	General strike smashed by Fascists
		October	Start of Fascist insurrection
			Mussolini invited to form government
			The 'March on Rome'

Points to consider

1) In what ways was the situation favourable to the growth of Fascism in post-war Italy?
2) What were Mussolini's tactics in the period 1919–October 1922?
3) Did Mussolini 'seize power'?
4) At what points between 1919 and October 1922 could Mussolini have been stopped?
5) What was Fascism?

4

THE PERIOD OF TRANSITION

A PARLIAMENTARY OR FASCIST STATE?

Until January 1925 the transformation of the Liberal and constitutional Italian state into a Fascist dictatorship proceeded in a muddled and uncertain way. At times it was difficult to say whether Mussolini was aiming at a dictatorship or merely at a more authoritarian government within the existing constitution. He had after all been invited by the King to form a parliamentary government, even though armed Fascists were in the process of seizing power throughout Italy, and like his predecessors, he had to negotiate a coalition with the potentially sympathetic parties in parliament. The situation was made even more ambiguous by the fact that the Fascist Party was, as the historian Philip Morgan has called it, 'a disparate alliance [which] was internally divided over both ends and means'. Some of the more moderate Fascists, or revisionists, wanted simply to make the existing Italian state more efficient, while the radicals in the squads and national syndicalist groups (Fascist trade unions) hoped for a real revolution that would in effect absorb the state into the Party.

Mussolini had to continue to lead this divided movement by trying to act as a mediator between the moderates and radicals. Thus he appeared alternately to take up extreme and moderate positions. Yet there is no doubt that he intended ultimately to establish a one-party state in which he would exercise supreme power, but in the first two years he had to move slowly so that he did not alarm his enemies sufficiently into uniting to stop him. He had, as he said, to pluck the chicken 'one feather at a time'!

MUSSOLINI'S FIRST YEAR IN POWER

Not only was Mussolini Prime Minister, but he also took over the key posts of both the Ministries of the Interior and Foreign Affairs. The post of Minister of the Interior was particularly important because it enabled him to control the Italian police forces. As the Fascist Party had only 35 seats in parliament, Mussolini's first task was to negotiate a coalition which would give him a sufficient majority to enable his government to survive. Thus out of the 15 members of his Cabinet only four were Fascists. The others were Liberals and *Popolari*, together with a general and an admiral. When parliament met on 16 November Mussolini addressed the chamber in an aggressive and hectoring manner:

> I could have made of this dull and grey hall a bivouac for corpses. I could have nailed up the doors of Parliament and have established an exclusively Fascist Government. I could have done those things, but at least for a time I did not do them. . . . I do not want, as long as I can avoid it, to rule against the Chamber; but the Chamber must feel its own position. That position opens the possibility that it may be dissolved in two days or in two years. We ask for full powers because we want to assume full responsibility. Without full powers you know very well we couldn't save one lira – I say one lira. We do not want to exclude the possibility of voluntary cooperation, for we will cordially accept it if it comes from deputies, senators or even from competent private citizens. Every one of us has a religious sense of our difficult task. The country cheers us and waits. We will not give it words, but facts. We formally and solemnly promise to restore the budget to health. And we will restore it. We want to make a foreign policy of peace, but at the same time one of dignity and steadiness. We will do it. We intend to give the Nation a discipline. We will give it. Let none of our enemies of yesterday, of today, of tomorrow, be illusioned in regard to our permanence in power . . .
>
> (*My Autobiography*, pp. 185–6)

Why then did this profoundly undemocratic speech not provoke a storm of protest? Many of the deputies and senators were convinced that Mussolini was the strong man that Italy needed. Giolitti, for instance, when he was asked to comment on Mussolini's speech, supported it and added that parliament had got the government it more than deserved. In the Senate the Liberal Senator, Albertini summed up the reasons why so many non-Fascists were ready to tolerate Mussolini:

> Mussolini has given to the government freshness, youth and vigour, and has won favour at home and abroad . . . he has saved Italy from the socialist danger which has been poisoning our life for twenty years.
>
> (Quoted in D. Mack Smith, *Italy: a Modern History*, University of Michigan Press, 1959, p. 374)

Mussolini's attacks on parliament were also supported by the Communists, who hoped that he would destroy the Liberal state and so prepare the way for a Russian-style revolution. Not surprisingly he gained an overwhelming vote of confidence in both chambers. Shortly afterwards they also agreed to grant Mussolini emergency powers for 12 months, which would allow him to raise taxes and govern Italy without having to secure the approval of parliament. He then proceeded over the next few months to arrest thousands of his political enemies and replace elected local government representatives by Fascists loyal to himself.

He certainly moved towards a more authoritarian and centralised government, and used violence on a considerable scale, but he nevertheless took care not to alarm his Liberal, Conservative and Catholic coalition partners. Thus to the disappointment and anger of many Fascists he did not immediately begin a Fascist revolution. Indeed he excluded all the leading Fascists from his Cabinet and at its first meeting announced policies some of which could have come from any Conservative or right-wing Liberal prime minister: the restoration of law and order within Italy and the need to balance the budget by making economies. Neither did he remove the civil servants, the generals, the judges and the police officers on whom the running of the state depended, largely because he was unable to replace them with men of sufficient ability from the ranks of his own followers.

This continuity in the administration also helped to convince Mussolini's coalition partners that he was primarily concerned with defending the existing social order rather than unleashing a revolution. Indeed on one level Mussolini's initial record did confirm this. Land reform was suspended, death duties reduced by half and the commission on wartime profits was dissolved. The Economics Minister, De Stefani, was allowed to implement a policy of denationalisation in order to liberate industry from government controls and monopolies. Mussolini similarly appeased the Church. He clamped down on anti-Catholicism in his own party and branded 'red atheism', or Communism, as the real enemy. He also inferred that, provided the Church backed his government, he would in turn give his support to proposals for a special Catholic university at Milan and the teaching of compulsory religious instruction in schools. Mussolini was anxious to drive a wedge between the *Popolari* Party, whose brand of Christian democracy he deeply distrusted even though they supported his coalition, and the more conservative Catholic heirarchy.

The role of the Party

For Mussolini the Party remained his real source of power. Its squads could alone neutralise the Socialists and Communists and enable Mussolini to make veiled threats to his coalition partners that ultimately if they did not support him he would unleash a reign of terror. Initially parliament was given plenty of evidence of this capability. Three opposition members were assassinated and some 50 others were attacked. Several political prisoners were mudered in jail, while other opponents were given a potentially fatal mixture of castor oil mixed with petrol. In November 1924 the *Manchester Guardian* calculated that over the previous year there had been an average of five such incidents a day. Yet, as we have seen, the potentially uncontrollable violence and ambitions of the Party were also a threat to Mussolini, who had to move carefully in consolidating his power so as to avoid a rupture with his allies. It was thus essential that Mussolini should be seen to be in control of the Party, while at the same time he had to be careful not to give its members the impression that he had become yet another constitutional politician. The moderate Fascists were strengthened by the merger of the Party with the Nationalists who had close links with the Italian civil service and judiciary. Together they formed the more moderate right wing of the Party, which believed in the preservation of the monarchy and the authority of the state.

Although Mussolini went nowhere near as far as the Fascist squads and syndicalists wanted in promoting a policy of 'fascistisation' of the state, he managed to strengthen the influence of the Fascist Party as a whole over the state whilst simultaneously tightening his own grip on the Party. In December 1922 he set up under his own chairmanship the Fascist Grand Council, on which all the key Fascist leaders sat, to coordinate government and Party policy. As chairman, his control of the Council was guaranteed since he could fix the agenda and co-opt new members whenever he wished. The Council rapidly began to undermine the independence of the Cabinet and reduce it to little more than a rubber stamp. The decisions to transfer from the King to Mussolini the right to call an election and to create the Fascist militia were both initially taken in the Grand Council and accepted by the Cabinet without argument. The creation of the militia was also an ambiguous measure which both imposed a new discipline on the Fascist squads by incorporating them into a national paramilitary organisation, and broke their local connections with the *ras*. However, the militia was firmly under the orders of Mussolini and not the King and thus became in effect a legal Party army paid for by the state to keep Fascism in power. Its existence showed all too clearly that Mussolini was ready to keep power by using force if it became necessary.

The Acerbo Electoral Law

Although Mussolini had only 35 seats in the Chamber, he did not rush to hold a general election despite the fact that many thought he would win a massive majority. He was more cautious and preferred not to risk the loss of prestige which would result from anything less than a landslide victory. First he had to reform the whole electoral system to ensure that his party would have a built-in advantage. Plans for this were discussed in the Grand Council, and in July 1923 the Acerbo Electoral Law was presented to parliament. It was a mixture of majority and proportional electoral systems. Any party which won a quarter of the votes would automatically receive two-thirds of the seats in the Chamber of Deputies. The remainder of the seats would then be divided proportionally among the other parties.

As it was a transparent scheme to ensure a massive Fascist victory, why did the Liberals vote to accept it? Mussolini did all he could to overawe the Chamber during the debate. The galleries were crowded with armed Fascists, who menacingly played with their daggers and revolvers, but it was not just fear that accounted for his victory. The Liberals hated the post-war proportional system which had greatly strengthened the Socialists and *Popolari*. Many also believed, like Salandra, that electoral reform in giving Mussolini a secure majority would help normalise or constitutionalise Fascism and lead it to abandon violence and revolution. The *Popolari* and the moderate Socialists under Bonomi disliked the bill, but decided to abstain from actually voting against it. Not surprisingly therefore the Chamber endorsed the Acerbo Law by the comfortable majority of 235 to 139 and the Senate by 165 to 41.

THE ELECTION OF APRIL 1924

Although Mussolini contemptuously referred to the election as a 'paper game', and stressed that 'fifty thousand guns are better than the support of five million voters', he did nevertheless make careful preparations for the campaign. Bribery and violence were used on a large scale. Voting forms were frequently seized from opponents and the names of the dead mysteriously appeared on the voting lists. The moderate Socialists were particularly singled out for attacks and intimidation by the Fascists, but sometimes the violence was indiscriminate. In Ferrara, for instance, Balbo advised his squads to seize the first elector to come out of the voting booth

> and break his head open – even if he has voted for us, too bad for him – shouting, 'Bastard, you voted for the Socialists'. In this way we can be sure that, after this example, no one will risk not voting for the *lista nazionale* (national list).
> (Quoted in P. Corner, *Fascism in Ferrara*, Oxford University Press, 1975, p. 263)

Altogether several hundred people were killed and several foreign journalists who dared expose what was going on were beaten up and thrown out of Italy. Yet officially Mussolini insisted that all this was not happening. As Mack Smith has so tellingly observed, 'the secret of success lay in obtaining the effects of violence, while maintaining the reputation of non-violence'!

Mussolini's campaign was also helped by the large number of Liberals and right-wing Catholics who applied to be put on the list of government candidates. In the event of the Fascists winning 25 per cent of the vote they would almost certainly be given a seat in the Chamber. The amalgamation of the Fascist Party with the Nationalists also greatly assisted Mussolini because it turned rivals into allies in the south where the Party had previously been very weak. Thanks to large-scale propaganda, bribery and the work of the prefects in the southern provinces, the local politicians began to see the Party with its connections to Mussolini as the sure way of getting government money and favours. Thus some 60 per cent of the official candidates in Sicily were Liberals, including some whom the local Fascist leader in Palermo had previously excluded on the grounds that they were members of the Mafia! Altogether the candidates on the Fascist electoral list won 65 per cent of the votes and 374 seats. Support was strongest in Emilia and Tuscany, the heartland of the squads, and in the south where Mussolini's victory was seen as the key to continued subsidies and favours. In Piedmont, Liguria, Lombardy and Venetia the government failed to gain an absolute majority over the other parties.

When parliament met, the government controlled 403 deputies, with a further 29 giving their qualified support. The opposition consisted of 39 *Popolari*, 25 moderate Socialists, 22 Maximalists (or more extreme Socialists), 19 Communists, one dissident Fascist and two members of the Sardinian Party of Action. Although widespread violence and corruption had undoubtedly increased the government's vote, Mussolini's victory did genuinely represent public opinion. After the revolutionary turmoil of the post-war years he was seen as the man who could both crush Communism and control the extremes of Fascism. The great Italian Liberal philosopher, Benedetto Croce, for instance, strongly urged his fellow Italians to vote for Fascism, although later he was to become its bitter critic.

THE MURDER OF GIACOMO MATTEOTTI

Even after the election Mussolini's ultimate aims still remained far from clear. Many 'normalisers' both within his own party and amongst his Liberal and right-wing allies assumed that his decisive electoral victory would enable him to legitimise Fascist power and end the acts of violence against its opponents. He would, they hoped, at last become a parliamentary and constitutional prime minister. He certainly surprised one journalist by suggesting that the Fascists should collaborate with all the parties, including the Socialists, but essentially he was not ready to disband the Fascist squads. Ominously his special murder detachment, the *Ceka*, composed of violent criminals, was booked into a hotel conveniently next to the Chamber of Deputies where it was paid daily by Mussolini's personal office. Its task was to eliminate deputies, by murder if necessary, who might still have the courage to criticise the irregularities of the recent election.

When parliament opened on 30 May Mussolini asked for the blanket approval of several thousand laws and that the million complaints about the election should be immediately dismissed. This astonishing request immediately drew criticism from the Socialist deputy Matteotti, who argued that the whole election result was invalid:

> Against the validity of this election, we present this pure and simple objection – that the . . . government, nominally with a majority of over four million . . . did not obtain these votes either in fact or freely . . . No Italian voter was free to decide according to his own will . . The Premier had entrusted the custody of the booths to the Fascist militiamen.
>
> (Quoted in R. Collier, *Duce!*, Collins, 1971, pp. 72–3)

When he finished his speech he then remarked, in response to the howls of rage and threats from the Fascists: 'I have made my speech – now you can prepare my funeral oration.' Sure enough on 10 June the *Ceka* murdered Matteotti and buried him in the countryside outside Rome. Publicly, of course, Mussolini denied all knowledge of the murder, but then in mid-August, thanks to information given to the police from a caretaker who had observed the activities of the *Ceka's* thugs, Matteotti's body was discovered and his murderers arrested. Matteotti's death could not be shrugged off by Mussolini as just another unofficial act of violence carried out by the squads. It was assumed both in parliament and outside – quite correctly in retrospect – that the *Ceka* was carrying out the express orders of Mussolini.

These revelations led to a major crisis which seriously threatened Mussolini's position and appeared to give the Italians one last chance of getting rid of Fascism. Yet this very possibility was also a moment of truth which made the King, the Vatican, the majority of the Senate and several other key institutions realise why they had supported Mussolini in the first place. They still feared the Left and above all believed, perhaps correctly, that if the Fascist government fell, it would not give up power quietly and would plunge Italy into civil war. Their fears were given some justification when Mussolini mobilised the Fascist militia to do the very work for which it had been set up – to defend the new regime.

Nevertheless Mussolini was initially pushed onto the defensive. He dismissed de Bono, the head of both the police and the militia, as well as his two lieutenants, Marinelli and Rossi, yet he himself managed to survive, thanks largely to the miscalculation of his opponents.

The Aventine seccession

At the end of June about 150 Socialists, Communists, Republicans and Liberal deputies decided to withdraw from parliament in protest against Mussolini's involvement in Matteotti's murder. They called themselves the Aventine seccession after the famous demonstration in ancient Rome against tyranny when the citizens retreated in protest to the Aventine hill outside the city. They claimed that only they represented the nation and that it was imperative that the Fascist regime should be overthrown, yet with the exception of the Communists they were unwilling to challenge Mussolini on the streets. They assumed that the King would dismiss Mussolini and appoint a new Cabinet which would then crack down on Fascist violence. In fact, however, neither the King, nor parliament nor the Council of Ministers moved against Mussolini. Many Liberals, like Croce, convinced themselves that Mussolini was now their prisoner and three members of Salandra's party even agreed to join a new Mussolini Cabinet. On 24 June the Senate gave him an overwhelming vote of confidence, which only 21 senators opposed. Any chance of the *Popolari* and the Socialists forming a new anti-Mussolini government was destroyed when the Pope withdrew his support from those *Popolari* deputies who had joined the Aventine. Although the Pope realised that Mussolini was at least partly responsible for Matteotti's murder, he valued the Fascists more as a barrier against Communism and Socialism.

MUSSOLINI'S DOUBLE POLICY

Although many of the more moderate Fascists, or 'timid and flabby fringes' as Mussolini called them in his autobiography, were leaving the Party in revulsion against Matteotti's murder, he had nevertheless to be careful that his concessions to parliament did not drive the *ras* and the squads into rebellion against his policies. Thus he had to continue his balancing act until he was finally forced to abandon all pretence of moderation in January 1925. On the one hand he told the National Council of the Fascist Party in August that violence was necessary in public life and that a strong government was more important than liberty, while on the other hand in a public speech in November he promised to control the violent side of Fascism and make the Party more democratically accountable. By December 1924 it was becoming increasingly difficult to reconcile these contradictory policies. Mussolini was facing opposition from both the moderate or normalising wing of the Party, who wanted the Aventine deputies recalled and a government of national reconciliation formed, and the *ras*, who feared that Mussolini had sold out to the Liberals.

At the end of the month he was plunged into a fresh crisis when a revealing memorandum was published in the Liberal newspaper, *Il Mondo*. It was written by Cesare Rossi, the former director of the Fascist Press Bureau, and implicated Mussolini personally in a long list of assaults and murders. The publication of the memorandum was a turning point in Italian politics. For a short time Mussolini completely lost the initiative and his Liberal ministers at last decided to resign from the Cabinet. By New Year's Eve the rumour was gaining ground in Italy that Mussolini had fallen, and in places there were enthusiastic celebrations to mark the end of Fascism. Finally his hand was forced when a delegation of the *ras* and the senior militia officers travelled up to Rome on 31 December and delivered an ultimatum to the effect that he should either forcefully impose a Fascist regime on Italy or else they would overthrow him and act independently. Their message was underlined by the eruption of large-scale Fascist rioting in Florence.

It was now quite clear that Mussolini could only remain in power by a show of force. He summoned parliament where, thanks to the Aventine seccession, he could still count on a majority and on 3 January 1925 defiantly told the Deputies:

I declare before all Italy that I assume full responsibility for what has happened. . . . If Fascism has turned out to be only castor oil and rubber truncheons instead of being a superb passion inspiring the best youth of Italy, I am responsible . . . Italy wants peace and quiet and to get on with its work. I shall give it all these, if possible in love, but if necessary by force. In the forty-eight hours after my speech the whole situation will be changed.

(*Italy: a Modern History*, p. 385)

This last statement was no empty threat. All over Italy Fascist squads closed down opposition newspapers and beat up opponents. The Fascist militia was mobilised and the police arrested key members of the opposition. By the end of January there was no doubt that Mussolini was firmly in control of Italy. The Fascist government had now become a 'regime', which might well survive for decades.

How was it that Mussolini was able to stage such a comeback when it seemed that he was on the verge of defeat? Crucial to his survival was King Victor Emmanuel's support. If he had demanded Mussolini's resignation, the *Duce* would have found it virtually impossible to remain in power. The army, the Conservatives and the higher ranks of the bureaucracy would have deserted him. Taking their cue from the King, the majority of the Liberals and Conservatives did not follow their leaders Giolitti, Salandra and Orlando into opposition, but instead in January rallied to the support of Mussolini. Essentially despite all that had happened they still believed that Fascism could be normalised and was in any case preferable to a left-wing government. Also of considerable importance in its effect was the tactical error that the opposition had made by withdrawing from parliament. This ensured that Mussolini could still dominate the Chamber.

timeline	1923	March	Pact of Fusion between Fascists and Nationalists
		July	Acerbo Electoral Law approved by Parliament
	1924	April	General Election
		June	Matteotti's murder
		December	The publication of Rossi's memorandum
	1925	January	Mussolini defends himself in a speech to parliament

Points to consider

1) To what extent was Italy still a liberal constitutional state during the period October 1922–January 1925?
2) How successfully did Mussolini manage to keep the balance between the Fascists and non-Fascists during this period?
3) Why was Mussolini able to obtain a majority for the Acerbo bill?
4) Why did the Matteotti murder and the Rossi revelations not lead to Mussolini's dismissal and the collapse of Fascism?

5

BUILDING THE TOTALITARIAN STATE
1925–9

MUSSOLINI AND TOTALITARIAN DICTATORSHIP

By 1929 Mussolini had so strengthened his position that only force could have removed him from power, yet he still had to compromise with the strong non-Fascist groups in Italian society, which had supported him in October 1922 and enabled him to survive the outcry caused by Matteotti's murder in June 1924. Over the next five years he made considerable progress towards creating a totalitarian dictatorship, but this was not primarily to be a dictatorship of the Fascist Party. The Fascist 'revolution' was to be carried out by the state aided by the Party, both of which were by now firmly under Mussolini's control. In October 1925 he used the following slogan to describe the totalitarian society he was trying to create in Italy: 'Everything within the state, nothing outside the state, nothing against the state'. His definition disappointed many of the hard-line Fascist leaders who assumed that it would be the Party that would dictate to the state rather than, as Mussolini seemed to be suggesting, the state to the Party. Increasingly as Mussolini was able to use the courts and the police to protect his regime, the Party took on the subordinate but nevertheless important social and educational role of winning over the Italian people to the ideas of Fascism.

a note on . . .

TOTALITARIANISM

In 1932 in an article in the *Italian Encyclopaedia* Mussolini stressed: '. . . for the Fascist, everything is in the state, and nothing human or spiritual exists, much less has value, outside the state. In this sense Fascism is totalitarian'. However, despite Mussolini's claims, Fascist Italy was never completely totalitarian, as Soviet Russia and even Nazi Germany were to be.

A totalitarian state is a one-party state in which all political, social, economic and cultural activities are controlled by the central government. As Count Yorck von Wartenburg, one of the unsuccessful conspirators against Hitler in 1944, observed, '. . . the essential element [of such a state] . . . is the total claim of the state on the citizen involving the elimination of his religious and moral objections towards God'. It is the exact opposite of a liberal, pluralistic society in which a number of political parties and religions co-exist and where the individual is within reason free to lead an independent life. A totalitarian state on the other hand aims to coordinate or control the activities of all organisations and persons so that they will work toward goals set out out for them by the 'Leader', or the *Duce* as Mussolini called himself.

THE 'DEFEAT' OF THE FASCIST PARTY

In January 1925 when Mussolini was pushed into action by an ultimatum from the Fascist Party and militia, it did seem that the Party had emerged as the single most powerful force in Italy. In February Farinacci, the hard-line *ras* of Cremona, was appointed the National Secretary of the Party. He lost little time in unleashing yet another wave of terror throughout Italy, directed not only against known opponents of Fascism in industry, the civil service and the various Catholic organisations, but also in some cases even against the new members of the Party itself who were judged to have joined after October 1922 purely because they thought that their career might benefit from membership. Farinacci passionately believed that the Party was the guardian and guarantor of the Fascist revolution and he aimed to create, as he put it later, 'the strictest dictatorship of the Party in the nation'. In other words the Party would be in a position to dictate to the state. Farinacci's ambitions, however, clashed with reality. Mussolini still needed the backing of the powerful conservative forces and institutions that had kept him in power since October 1922 – the landowners, industrialists, the bankers, the armed forces and the professional middle classes. There could be no question of the Fascist Party itself seizing the initiative, and consequently Mussolini had to use the existing institutions of the state to create the Fascist dictatorship. Parliament rubber-stamped the necessary laws and then it was the civil service, the judges and the police who enforced them.

Inevitably, then, Mussolini had to act to defeat or at least curb the ambitions of the Party. In June 1925 he called a Party conference where he announced that the Party should aim at the 'fascistisation' of every aspect of Italian life, but it was nevertheless made very clear that it must obey orders imposed from above. Debates were cut short and the conference was terminated after only a few hours instead of lasting the three days, originally scheduled for it. In October 1925 when Fascists in Florence embarrassed Mussolini by publicly beating up alleged Freemasons in front of foreign tourists, he decided to dissolve the squads and purge the Florentine Fascists of their more extreme members. A few months later Farinacci was replaced by the *ras* of Brescia, Augusto Turati, whose task was to tame the Party and to ensure that it took its orders from the state. About 60 000 ex squad members and veteran Fascists, together with the more extreme *ras* were expelled and largely replaced by government bureaucrats, who joined for the most part to keep their jobs. In October 1926 internal party democracy, which involved elections to all party posts, was abolished and the Party had to accept candidates, loyal to Mussolini, who were nominated by Turati's office. From now on the Party was tightly controlled from the centre and integrated into the Fascist state. Mussolini made this very clear in his circular to the prefects (provincial governors) of 5 January 1927:

> I solemnly reaffirm that the prefect is the highest authority of the state in the province. He is the direct representative of the central executive power. All citizens, and in particular those having the great privilege and supreme honour of supporting Fascism, owe respect and obedience to the highest political representative of the Fascist regime and must work under him to make his task easier.

Whenever necessary, the prefect must stimulate and harmonise the various activities of the party . . . The party and its members from the highest to the lowest, now that the revolution is complete, are only a conscious instrument of the will of the state whether at the centre or the periphery . . .

Now that the state is equipped with all its own methods of prevention and repression there are some 'residues' that must disappear. I am speaking of *squadrisimo* [the Fascist squads] which in 1927 is simply anachronistic, sporadic, but which reappears in an undisciplined fashion during periods of public commotion. These illegal activities must stop . . . the era of reprisals, destruction and violence is over . . . the prefects must prevent this happening by using all means at their disposal, I repeat by using all means at their disposal . . .'

(Quoted in A. Aquarome, *L'organizzaziore dello stato totalitario*, Einaudi, 1965, pp. 485–6)

The machinery of repression

What remained of the old liberal state was swept away in two distinct phases of legislation between November 1925 and October 1926, the official justifications for which were four separate attempts to assassinate Mussolini. His government was immensely strengthened by a whole series of emergency laws, which were skilfully drafted by Alfredo Rocco, the Minister of Justice. These gave the government the power to eliminate virtually all opposition and to set up a police state. By the Law of Associations (25 November 1925) state officials could be banned from joining any organisation of which the state disapproved. Further legislation allowed the government to deprive the Aventine and Communist MPs of their parliamentary seats, and brought journalists firmly under the control of the government. The notorious Law for the Defence of the State reintroduced the death penalty for attempts on the life of the royal family and Mussolini and drew up a list of tough punishments against anybody trying to revive a banned party or association. To enforce this a special tribunal was created, which was specifically instructed by Rocco to mete out 'swift and severe' justice. Political prisoners convicted by this court of more serious charges were then sent to penal settlements on Lipari and other remote islands off the toe of Italy. Even a spontaneous joke about Mussolini made, for instance, in a café, could lead some unfortunate individual to be exiled for several years in an isolated village in southern Italy. Mussolini saw this as an essential task of 'social hygiene'.

In 1927 Arturo Bocchini, the Chief of the Security Police, set up a new political police force, the *OVRA* whose job was to investigate and spy on any activity which was hostile to the Fascist state. By the early 1930s *OVRA* was carrying out some 20 000 investigations a week. As Philip Morgan put it, 'policing increasingly came to involve information-gathering and comment on practically everything that talked or moved'.

Workers, employers and corporatism

'Corporatism' was one of the most important parts of Fascist ideology. It was constantly presented as a middle way between the extremes of Communism and Capitalism. The corporations were organisations which were theoretically supposed to include both employers and workers of a particular industry or trade. It was assumed that both groups would cooperate harmoniously to solve labour and business problems and that this would result in greater productivity. In 1929 Mussolini triumphantly announced that the setting up of the corporations had completely ended the class conflict between capital and labour and that both sides were working together with total equality of rights and duties, yet much of this was propaganda particularly for foreign consumption. The reality was different and favoured the employers rather than the workers. Mussolini's replacement of the liberal constitutional state by a Fascist dictatorship had been accompanied by the growing suppression of the Communist, Socialist and Catholic trade unions and workers' rights to protest and to strike. His dictatorship had only been made possible by the support of the Italian industrialists and upper classes who feared Socialism and Communism more than Fascism. Thus he was careful to ensure that in any settlement with the Fascist syndicates or trade unions he must safeguard and perhaps even strengthen the employers' rights and reserve for himself the ultimate power to make the key decisions. This clashed with the ambitions of Edmondo Rossi, the leader of the National Confederation of Fascist Syndicates, who wanted a system of 'mixed syndicates' or corporations in which both employers and workers would be represented. These would be controlled by the Fascist Party and all other unions or employers' organisations dissolved.

In 1924–5 the Fascist syndicates fought hard for the support of the workers and took part in several strikes. Initially their militancy was strengthened by Farinacci's campaign against those few businessmen and industrialists who still had reservations about supporting Fascism. Nevertheless the weakness of the syndicates was exposed during a major strike by the metal workers in Brescia where the majority of the workers followed the leadership of the Socialist-controlled Federation of Metalworkers. It was clear that without the backing of the state the Fascist syndicates were too weak to compete with their rivals. Eventually the syndicates did receive the necessary support, and the strike was ended through negotiations between the government, the Party and the employers. The Federation of Metalworkers was completely excluded from the discussions.

Afterwards Mussolini was careful to purge the more militant Fascist syndicalist leaders. The way was then open for an agreement with the employers. By the Palazzo–Vidoni Pact the industrial employers' group (the *Confindustria*) conceded that the syndicates should become the sole representation of organised labour and that they would not negotiate with any other union. In return the employers then insisted on abolishing the elected factory councils and made clear that the syndicates had no authority within the factories. This agreement was given the force of law in April 1926. When Alfredo Rocco announced it in parliament, he stressed that 'the regulation of trade unions must be a means of disciplining them, not a means of creating powerful, uncontrollable bodies that can dominate the state'. It was apparent, therefore, that the law did not deal with both the workers and employers in an even-handed way. They were not combined into single corporations, although there was a voluntary provision (which was ignored in practice for setting up organs of cooperation between the employers and the syndicates. The employers were still independently represented by their organisation, the *Confindustria*. The law did make both strikes and lockouts illegal, but without strikes employers would hardly need to use the threat of a lockout. An arbitration court was also set up to deal with labour disputes, but as it consisted of a judge and two legal experts helped by advisers who all had to have university degrees, workers with real experience of industrial disputes were excluded.

Although the corporatist idea continued, largely for propaganda reasons, to be pursued by Mussolini, in practice he never seriously challenged the rights of the employers. According to one economic historian, R. Sarti, 'the industrial leadership of Italy dealt with Fascism as a hedgehog deals with a fox'. In other words the industrialists concentrated single-mindedly – and successfully – on protecting their right to manage their own factories and enterprises.

In July 1926 a Ministry of Corporations was set up. Mussolini was theoretically in charge but it was in fact run by the Under-Secretary, Giuseppe Bottai who believed passionately in creating mixed organisations of workers and employers. A year later Bottai produced the Charter of Labour, which was even called 'the Magna Carta of Fascism'. While it defined workers' rights in the areas of employment, social insurance and welfare provision, in deference to the *Confindustria* they were not made legally binding on employers.

In November 1928 Bottai made another effort to develop corporatism by breaking up the large National Confederation of Workers' Syndicates, which numbered some three million members, into several workers' associations. These corresponded exactly to the employers' associations in industry, farming and the services. Far from encouraging corporatism this merely weakened the workers still further by destroying their united base. Only in 1934 were 22 proper 'mixed corporations' at last set up containing representatives of the Party, employers, technical experts and workers. These were given the power to fix wage scales, settle labour disputes and advise generally on economic issues, but again in reality their main value was to act as propaganda for the regime in its effort to impress the world that it had found a third way between capitalism and communism. It only created yet more jobs for civil servants. To one of the exiled leaders of the Italian Communist Party, Palmiro Togliatti, corporatism was clearly a sham aimed at suppressing the workers:

> What is the structure of a corporation? It is based on 'equal' representation of the employers and of the employees, of the technical experts and of the Fascist Party. This 'equality' is only an illusion, as we have already seen, even if the employees' representatives . . . were truly representatives of the workers, the upper hand would still be given to the bosses by the

representatives of the Fascist Party and the technical experts. There is only one president of the corporations: Mussolini. (Quoted in P. Togliatti, *Lectures on Fascism,* London, 1976, p. 101)

MUSSOLINI AND THE CHURCH

Before 1914 Mussolini had bitterly attacked the Church as a servant of capitalism. Deep within himself he also despised the Christian virtues of humility and charity. As late as 1920 he had called Christianity 'detestable', but he rapidly came to appreciate that the Catholic Church was still immensely strong in Italy and could not be destroyed or taken over in the same way as the political parties and trade unions. It was for this reason that he sought to come to terms with it and ultimately to negotiate a compromise which would allow both Fascism and Catholicism to co-exist. In propaganda terms the advantages of this would be considerable. He would be able to claim Papal support for his regime and would be the first Italian statesman since the unification of Italy to sign an agreement with the Papacy.

During his first few years in power, therefore, even while the Fascist squads were attacking the Popolari Party and the Catholic trade unions, Mussolini took good care to keep on the right side of the Pope. For instance he found the money to increase priests' salaries and to make generous grants for repairing old churches. The Pope, too, was ready to come to terms with the new regime and anxious to negotiate an agreement that would enable the Church to survive. He was particularly worried about the impact of the Fascist youth movement, the National Balilla Organisation, which was determined to organise and to indoctrinate the whole of Italy's youth between the ages of 8 and 17, and hoped that an agreement with Mussolini might be able to safeguard the independence of the Church's own youth organisation, Catholic Action.

---

a note on . . .

THE PAPACY AND THE ITALIAN STATE SINCE 1860

The aloofness of the Papacy dated back to 1860 when Pope Pius IX had bitterly opposed Italian unification, as it had reduced the Papal States to what was called the Patrimony of St Peter, a narrow strip of land along the western coast of Italy, including Rome. In 1849 Rome had been occupied by French troops, following an appeal from Pius IX to crush the revolutionary Roman Republic led by Mazzini, and they effectively guaranteed the Pope's independence of the Italian state until they were withdrawn in 1870 when the Franco-Prussian war broke out. Italian troops then moved in to occupy the city and in July 1871 Rome became the capital of Italy. The government attempted to regulate the position of the Papacy by the Law of Guarantees, which gave the Pope complete diplomatic freedom in recognition of his role as head of the Catholic Church and allowed him to remain in the Vatican. The Papacy however refused both to recognise the validity of this law and indeed the sovereignty of the Italian state itself.

Negotiations were completed in early 1929 and the Lateran Pacts, which consisted of three agreements: a treaty, a financial convention and a concordat, were signed on 11 February. The independence of the Vatican City was recognised, financial compensation was granted to the Papacy for the loss of the Papal States in 1860–70, and through the Concordat the special position of the Church in Italian Society was acknowledged. Religious education was now allowed in secondary schools and the existence of Catholic Action was to be tolerated.

For Mussolini the propaganda value of the Lateran Agreements was great. He had negotiated a settlement with the Papacy, which had eluded all his predecessors since 1870 and which led to the recognition of Italy's sovereignty, and in return had apparently won the Church's support for Fascism. However, the continued existence of a strong independent Catholic Church with its own secondary schools, youth organisations and Catholic student movement represented by far the most serious potential challenge to the claims of the totalitarian Fascist state. As Martin Clark has pointed out, the Catholic youth movement 'mocked any claim that the *Duce* was rearing a new Fascist generation'.

THE EVOLUTION OF THE FASCIST CONSTITUTION

By 1929 it was quite clear that while Mussolini still needed political allies, he had become the strongest force in Italy. In December 1925 he had himself declared Head of Government and was no longer responsible to parliament. Only the King could now dismiss him. His position was further strengthened in January 1926 when he was allowed to make laws simply by decree, which would later be rubber-stamped by parliament. However, between 1925 and 1929 only some 45 out of 5533 laws were in fact discussed by parliament. Thus by this date Mussolini had combined in his position as Head of Government both executive and legislative powers. The Cabinet became increasingly unimportant and was only occasionally consulted by Mussolini. In December 1928 it was virtually replaced by the Grand Council of the Fascist Party, which was made an official organ of state. Not only did the Grand Council control the Party and after 1929 nominate its senior members, but it was also given the power to put forward names for appointments to posts in the Cabinet and ultimately to appoint Mussolini's successor. This was a major challenge to the powers of the King as head of state as it vested in the Council the necessary constitutional powers to guarantee the continuity of Fascism after the death of Mussolini. Increasingly he also took over control of the state ministries. By 1929 he was theoretically the minister in charge of eight departments out of a total of 13.

In November 1926 all political parties except the Fascists were abolished and in May 1928 parliament was radically reformed. There were to be no longer direct elections, but instead membership of the Chamber of Deputies was to be made up of 400 representatives specially chosen by the Grand Council from a list of 1000 names put forward by the syndicates and other Fascist organisations. The voters would then only be able to accept or reject these names as a single entirety. Parliament was dissolved without any opportunity to debate this new law, which, as Mussolini himself said, was 'without parallel in the history of the world'. Predictably in the subsequent election 98.4 per cent of the voters endorsed the party list, while only 135 773 people dared vote against it, but over a million boycotted the 'election'.

Democracy at local level had been abolished in 1926 when the elected local mayors were replaced by specially nominated *podesta* or Fascist local government officials. Most of these officials were in fact recruited from the ranks of the landowners who had controlled local government before 1919. In this way it has been argued that Mussolini rewarded his conservative supporters for their backing during the crucial period of 1922–5.

MUSSOLINI AS *DUCE*

Mussolini's power was underpinned by the constant propaganda campaign carried out by the Party and through the media. It justified his dictatorship by arguing that the central control of the nation by one man made for much greater efficiency. From this followed the cult of the *Duce* as a god-like being for whom no task was too great. It was even claimed that through willpower alone he had halted the flow of lava on Mt Etna before it had engulfed a village! Mussolini instructed the press to emphasise how hard he worked and how little sleep he needed. Simultaneously he was to be depicted as a great sportsman who could ride, play tennis and fence to a very high standard. He used to demonstrate his physical fitness by running up and down lines of troops when he inspected units of the army. By 1926 Turati, the Party Secretary, the Fascist journalists, Giusseppe Bottai and Arnaldo Mussolini (the dictator's brother and editor of *Il Popolo d'Italia*), were particularly concerned with creating the cult of the all-powerful and all-knowing *Duce*. His picture appeared on public buildings and he was regularly compared favourably with most of the geniuses in world history. Teachers particularly had to impress their pupils with his importance and almost god-like status. In one primary school exercise book for instance a child wrote:

> Among the people I love in this world I feel I love the *Duce* very much. He has made Italy free and strong and where before there were marshes, malaria and mosquitos and woodland he as if by magic, has made so many little blue houses rise up and the green countryside. He has founded Fascism which is order, discipline and strength. Everyone envies us our fine *Duce*! He is handsome, clever and good and he thinks about everyone from new born babies to the very old.
>
> (Quoted in G. Biondi and F. Imberciadori, . . . *Voi siete la primavera . . . l'ideologia fascista nel monda della scuola, 1925–1943*, Einaudi, 1982, p. 167)

The reality was very different. Although Mussolini made a show of exerting total control over the machinery of government and being concerned with even the smallest detail, the burden of day-to-day administration in the numerous ministries he directly controlled fell to the Under-Secretaries. As these lacked any political power they could not make the vital decisions which Mussolini himself failed to take. In crucial areas such as the armed forces important reforms were never implemented, with fatal results for the future. Mussolini's skills as a politician lay in his ability to exploit favourable opportunities, which he did brilliantly during the years 1921–9. However, the myth of the all-knowing *Duce* in time made him complacent and destroyed his political judgement.

timeline	1925	January	Alfredo Rocco appointed Minister of Justice
		June	Last Party Congress
		October	Palazzo–Vidoni Pact
		December	Mussolini calls himself 'Head of Government'
	1926	April	Law on the Judicial Regulation of Labour Relations
		July	Ministry of Corporations created
	1927	January	Party circular to prefects insisting that the Party is the instrument of the state's will
	1928	May	Act reshaping the Chamber of Deputies
	1929	February	Lateran Agreements

Points to consider

1) **To what extent can it be argued that the Fascist Party was 'defeated' during the years 1925–9?**
2) **Did Mussolini really establish a totalitarian state in Italy between 1925 and 1929?**
3) **Who gained more from the Lateran Agreements: Mussolini or the Pope?**
4) **How effectively did Mussolini consolidate his position during the period 1925–9?**
5) **'More than anything else the labor policies of the Fascist regime made its claims to being revolutionary a mockery.' (E. R. Tannenbaum). Do you agree with this assessment?**

6

THE FASCISTISATION OF ITALY

A CONSERVATIVE DICTATORSHIP?

By 1929 Mussolini had consolidated his power and established a dictatorship which essentially relied on the traditional machinery of the Italian state, the police, the courts, the individual ministries and the civil service rather than the Party. The power of the Left and of the trade unions had been broken, while big business and industry and the more conservative forces in the state, the smaller employers, the army, the landowners and the Church, not only benefited from the destruction of their political enemies, but also retained a considerable amount of freedom for themselves. Mussolini thus appeared to have established a conservative dictatorship. Was this his intention? E. R. Tannenbaum, for instance, argues that Mussolini was interested only 'in personal power and not in making a revolution or otherwise'. He was, as has been seen, a formidable politician who did not hesitate to compromise to cling on to power, but it would not be accurate to call him a supporter of the status quo by 1929. Although he had no precise revolutionary timetable for the future, he talked freely of Fascism as being a 'permanent revolution', and 1922 as marking the beginning of 'a profound political, moral, social revolution that in all probability will leave nothing or almost nothing of the past still in existence'. Mussolini's aims to mobilise the masses to support Fascism and then prepare Italy for an era of total war were certainly revolutionary in that this would involve the ruthless welding together of all classes and regions in Italy to form one united whole. His instrument for accomplishing the 'fascistisation' of Italian society was the Party, purged of its more radical members, and the Party's auxiliary organisations: the welfare agencies, workers' recreation clubs, the syndicates, the various youth and women's organisations and the Radio Agency. The Great Depression was to provide him with a perfect opportunity to start work on this process of 'fascistisation'.

THE IMPACT OF FASCISM ON PRIMARY AND SECONDARY EDUCATION

In the long term education mixed with a large dose of propaganda was as vital as terror and coercion in maintaining the grip of Fascism on Italy. Mussolini explained his own aims to the German writer and journalist, Emil Ludwig:

> The whole country had to become a great school for perpetual political education which would make the Italians into complete Fascists, new men, changing their habits, their way of life, their mentality, their character and finally, their physical make-up. It would no longer be a question of grumbling against the sceptical mandolin-playing Italians, but rather of creating a new kind of man who was tough, strong-willed, a fighter, a latter day legionary of Caesar for whom nothing was impossible.
>
> (Quoted in A. E. Ludwig, *Colloqui con Mussolini*, Milan, 1950, p. 111)

The first attempt to reform the Italian educational system was carried out by the Education Minister, Giovanni Gentile, in 1923. Although Mussolini enthused that it was 'the most Fascist of reforms', in fact his measures were academic and highly traditional. They neglected elementary and technical schools and paid most attention to the academic grammar schools and to creating an intellectual élite. They were almost immediately criticised by many Fascists for being too conservative and élitist and for hindering the very social mobility which would help unite a Fascist Italy.

Over the next 14 years there were eight ministers of education who all attempted to make education and schools more effective instruments of Fascism. All teachers at school and university had to swear oaths of loyalty to Mussolini. The administration of the education system was taken out of the hands of the local authorities and centralised. New Fascist textbooks were written and in the early 1930s their use became compulsory. All without exception stressed the omnipotent *Duce*, whose words of wisdom were constantly quoted. There was also much less emphasis on academic work in the new curriculum. In 1925 Mussolini stressed that

> There is no need to swamp [the pupils'] minds with past learning . . . Learning can be nothing more than a special indispensable kind of Swedish gymnastics for developing the brain and the sooner its useless superficial details are forgotten the more useful it will be. What is really necessary is that the schools should develop the character of the Italians.
>
> (Quoted in . . . *Voi siete la primavera . . . l'ideologia fascista nel mondo della scuola*, 1925–1943, p. 92)

One particularly important way of doing that was to enforce close cooperation between the elementary schools and the Fascist youth movement, the National Balilla Organisation, which was set up in 1926 to train children and teenagers in physical education and war games. Its influence on schools rapidly grew. For two years, 1928–30, it actually took over the management of nurseries and the village schools. In 1935 Balilla activities were introduced into the secondary school curriculum together with a much greater emphasis on military training. The whole educational system was then further reformed by Bottai when he unveiled the new Schools' Charter to the Fascist Grand Council in January 1939. It envisaged breaking down the barriers between academic and practical studies which were to become part of the curriculum for every school class. New schools were to be set up for the children of peasants and craftsmen to give them a realistic technical training. Clearly the whole aim of these reforms was to help mould the future Fascist citizens of Italy.

If these reforms had not been interrupted by war they would in time have had considerable influence. As it was the Fascist impact on the educational system was limited. Illiteracy did slowly decline and the number of pupils in secondary education increased, but Bottai's attempts to build up the prestige of the the vocational and scientific schools failed. The middle classes continued to send their children to the traditional grammar schools and Church schools, where Latin was still the main subject.

FASCISM AND THE UNIVERSITIES

Most students chose to study traditional subjects like History and Classics. Ironically, although the university population doubled in the 1930s Italy in fact trained fewer engineers, scientists and doctors than it had in the early 1920s.

University students were of crucial importance for the future of Fascism. The Fascist Student Organisation (GUF) was directly controlled by the Party and was supposed to rear the new Fascist intellectual élite. The membership was composed of predominantly male and female students between 18 and 28. As a potential élite they were encouraged to publish newspapers, make films and debate in relative freedom. One of the most popular activities was the Student Games which took place annually between 1934 and 1940. A popular aspect of these were debates in which students were allowed, as a safety valve, to criticise the Fascist regime. The best debaters and performers were given prizes and then shortlisted for posts in the Party. The majority of students did join the GUF if only because of its cultural facilities such as film clubs. Membership could also help their careers later in teaching or the civil service. The only independent student movement permitted by Mussolini as a consequence of the Lateran Agreements was the Federation of Catholic Students. This consciously set out to create an intellectual Catholic counter-élite which would defend the Church's interests.

THE YOUNG FASCISTS

Of course only a minority of Italy's youth was in the GUF. The Party bitterly resented the fact that the Balilla Organisation, whose potential influence was far greater, remained the responsibility of the Ministry of Education. Partly to by-pass what it called this 'lazy bourgeois bureaucracy' and to fill a genuine gap in the provisions for the organisation of youth, it set up the Young Fascists Organisation, in October 1930. This concentrated on young people between 18 and 21 who were already at work in factories or on the farms or who were studying at trade or vocational schools. They were given military training by the Fascist militia and brainwashed by political courses on the glories of Fascism. Their motto, 'Believe, Obey, Fight', was the key to the character of the new Fascist man Mussolini wanted to create. The Young Fascists tried to model themselves on the aggressive behaviour of the original Fascist squads during the years 1921–4, particularly when they attacked their rivals, the Catholic youth clubs.

Italian Youth of the Lictors

In 1937 the Party at last established its control over Italian youth when the Balilla and the Young Fascists were combined into one single movement, the Italian Youth of the Lictors (GIL), the main objective of which was to ensure that all young people in Italy between the ages of 6 and 21 were educated as future citizens of Fascist Italy. It was responsible for the provision of physical education in primary schools, for pre-military training and a large number of other courses. Through its summer camps and Saturday parades it did reach the majority of Italy's youth, but whether these young people were actually turned into convinced Fascists is a matter of debate. In 1934 the Party Secretary in Savona observed that 'The *Fasci Giovanili* [Young Fascists] were a joke from all points of view . . . Discipline did not exist and I was forced to resort to . . . severe punishments to get them to show up at meetings.' (Quoted in *State Control in Fascist Italy*, p. 116)

WELFARE AND LEISURE ACTIVITIES

To secure the Fascist regime in Italy Mussolini also needed to control and influence the great mass of the people. In 1925 the National Afterwork Agency or *Dopolavoro* (OND) was set up originally under the Ministry of National Economy. Its task was to take over the various workers' leisure clubs created by the syndicates or even originally by the Socialists. In 1927 it became the direct responsibility of the Party. Most large factories and offices made premises available for the OND to set up sporting facilities and club houses where there was usually a library, a radio and provision for showing films. By offering these cheap leisure facilities the OND was to a certain extent able to cushion the workers from the negative consequences of Mussolini's battle for the lira (see Chapter 7).

In 1931 Mussolini announced his new policy of 'going out to the people' and reaching those very large sections of the population which appeared indifferent to Fascism. In this campaign the OND played a key part by expanding its cutural and recreational roles. It organised, for instance, local festivals and arranged for travelling films and theatres to tour the country. By 1939 it was running an ambitious programme involving holiday camps and, with the help of subsidised rail fares, trips to the sea and the Alps for the city-bound workers. It essentially set out to provide entertainment and leisure rather than instruction in Fascist ideology. For Mussolini 'the important thing [was] that people are able to meet in places where we can control them'. The OND was moderately successful in achieving this. By 1939 40 per cent of all industrial workers and over 80 per cent of all state and private-sector salaried employees were members.

THE ROLE OF WOMEN AND THE 'BATTLE FOR BIRTHS'

By the late 1920s Mussolini, who was anxious to increase the population so that there would be sufficient soldiers for the future and a constant stream of settlers to the colonies, had developed very definite views about the role of women in Fascist Italy. He pronounced, for instance that 'war is to man what motherhood is to women'. Yet initially Fascism had supported female emancipation. Its programme of 1919 had promised women political equality, and in 1925 they were actually given the vote in local elections, although a year later local democracy was abolished. In 1927 Mussolini officially began a national campaign, or 'battle', to increase the birthrate and as a necessary precondition of this to persuade women to stay at home and be mothers and housewives. To set an example he brought his family to Rome to live with him and even fathered two more children. He also insisted on levying a tax on bachelors and both private employers and the civil service were ordered to employ family men as far as possible. Divorce was banned and the contraction of syphilis was made a criminal offence. His target was to raise the Italian population from 40 to 60 million by the 1950s. The Party also attempted to organise women in the service of Fascism. In 1935 it set up the Rural Housewives' Organisation and there was also a special Fascist Women's Movement within the Party which numbered some 500 000 by 1939.

Mussolini's attempt to turn back the clock failed. Women still continued to work in factories and study in higher education. Indeed in 1936 some 28 per cent of the industrial work force was female, while 15 per cent of the students at universities were also female. Similarly the 'battle of births' failed to produce the desired increase and by 1950 there were only 47.5 million Italians.

THE PARTY AND THE GREAT DEPRESSION

Far from weakening the grip of the Party on Italy the Depression of 1929–33 in fact enabled it to strengthen its influence over whole regions and classes of the population which had previously remained uninfluenced by it. The Party launched a major welfare programme, which was trumpeted by Mussolini as a policy for mobilising the whole country to help the victims of the Depression. The Party forced employers and workers' syndicates and the banks to donate a percentage of their profits, wages and salaries to its Agencies for Welfare Activities (EOAs). Throughout Italy the EOAs coordinated the distribution of financial relief for the unemployed in a methodical and thorough way. Each area was divided into subsections and then further broken down into the 'nuclei' of individual streets. Through the EOAs the Party really did reach the people. In the winter of 1934–5, for instance, about three million Italians were in receipt of regular daily welfare. De Felice, the controversial Italian biographer of Mussolini, sees the years 1929–34 as the period when both the Fascist regime and the *Duce* enjoyed their greatest popularity and security.

FASCISTISATION ACCELERATES, 1936–40

One of the greatest of Mussolini's triumphs was the brief and victorious war of 1935–6 which ended in the annexation of Ethiopia (see Chapter 8). The victory inevitably strengthened Mussolini's own position and seemingly vindicated the whole Fascist regime, thus leading to an acceleration in the pace of the fascistisation of Italy. Many historians believe it was during this period that the real Fascist revolution occurred when Mussolini strove hardest to inculcate in the Italians a belief that they were a master race destined to rule an empire. In 1938 he told his son-in-law Ciano that:

> Henceforth the revolution must impinge upon the habits of the Italians. They must learn to be less sympathetic in order to become hard, relentless and hateful – in other words masters.
> (Quoted in P. Morgan, *Italian Fascism, 1919–1945*, Macmillan, 1995, p. 158)

Over a wide area the regime became much more confident in its efforts to control and brainwash the Italian people. Significantly, for instance, the Ministry of Press and Propaganda was renamed the Ministry of Popular Culture in May 1937 and clearly had ambitions of creating a new mass Fascist culture. Symbolically plans were drawn up for building a 'Mussolini forum' in Rome, that was to contain an enormous bronze statue 80 metres high which would have the body of Hercules and the face of Mussolini. In 1938 the new Fascist salute was introduced and all official communications had to end with the words 'Long live the *Duce*'.

The anti-bourgeois campaign

To a certain extent this new wave of Fascism was reminiscent of the era of the revolutionary squads during the years 1920–2. Mussolini was becoming increasingly critical of the prosperous middle classes (the bourgeoisie), whom he saw as half-hearted, unheroic and far too fond of their comforts. Once in an unguarded moment he even went so far as to say that at least 80 per cent of the bourgeoisie would have to be destroyed. By the late 1930s foreign observers certainly thought that he was moving to the Left again and reported that Italian bankers and businessmen were becoming worried. It is true that there were some attacks on privilege and capitalism in the Fascist student journals, and in October 1939 the syndicates were allowed to appoint factory agents to represent them on the shop floor in large factories. Yet Mussolini was not really interested in targeting 'bourgeois' wealth and the private sector of the economy. Rather his campaign was directed against the 'bourgeois mentality', which was seen as decidedly unfascist, cosmopolitan and degenerate.

Anti-semitism and racism

The anti-bourgeois campaign was also the context in which Mussolini published, to the considerable surprise of the Italian people and of his own officials, the Race Manifesto of July 1938. This had been drawn up on his instructions by the Ministry of Popular Culture. It argued that:

> The populatia of present day Italy is of Aryan origin . . . The Jews do not belong to the Italian race . . . The Jews represent the only people that have never been assimilated in Italy and that is because they are composed of non-European racial elements, absolutely different from those which produced Italians.
>
> (Quoted in R. De Felice, *Mussolini il Duce, ii*, Einaudi, 1981, pp. 866–74)

Between September and November 1938 a series of race laws were enacted: foreign-born Jews who had immigrated to Italy since 1919 were deprived of their citizenship, mixed marriages were banned, the civil service, army and Party purged of Jews, and Jewish children were excluded from schools and forbidden to mix with 'Aryans'.

To most contemporaries including the Pope, and indeed many historians since, the prime reason for Mussolini's anti-semitic campaign was to signal to Hitler that he was serious about realigning Italy fully with Nazi Germany. Yet it was not just foreign policy that dictated his anti-semitic campaign. To him the supposedly international outlook and connections of the Jews made them typical members of the materialistic middle classes. He argued that the creation of a Jewish national home in Palestine proved that the Jews had a divided loyalty which would be dangerous in war. His anti-semitism was also part of a wider racial policy aimed at introducing *apartheid* into Italy's colonial empire in Africa, which he thought essential if Italy was to rule 'subject races'.

The Chamber of Fasces and Corporations

In January 1939 the 'fascistisation' of Italy made further progress when the Chamber of Deputies was replaced by the Chamber of Fasces and Corporations. The new legislation greatly strengthened the executive as the Chamber was now made up of members of the National Council of the Party, the Corporations and the Fascist Grand Council, who were simply appointed by the government. The only remaining constitutional organs which were not yet 'fascistised' were the Crown and the Senate.

HOW POPULAR WAS THE FASCIST REGIME?

Outright hostility to Mussolini and the Fascist regime was rare. The outlawing of the political parties and the surveillance of OVRA ensured that opposition was limited to the occasional circulation of anti-Fascist literature, either spread by small groups within Italy or smuggled across the frontier from emigrants in Switzerland and France. The only overt opposition to Mussolini was provided by the non-Italian populations in South Tyrol and Venezia Giulia, which were both acquired by Italy in 1919. Despite the existence of some 228 000 Germans in South Tyrol and 327 000 Slovenians and 98 000 Croats in Venezia Giulia, the Fascist government insisted on a policy of complete Italianisation. Even inscriptions on tombstones had to be changed. Not surprisingly the local priests led a stubborn cultural resistance and in Venezia Giulia a terrorist campaign was mounted against Italian teachers and officials.

In Italy itself support or at least tolerance of Mussolini grew until 1937 or even 1938. The welfare agencies and the OND made life tolerable for the working classes and Mussolini's regime had provided a degree of stability that shielded Italy from the worst of the Depression. It was only in 1938 that this tolerance began to be eroded when Fascism started to interfere in the minutiae of private life. The Italians were, for instance, ordered to drop the use of the informal 'you' – '*Lei*' – in favour of the more formal '*Voi*'. Even the design of their clothes and bathing suits was subject to political control. The alliance with Germany was also unpopular as it seemed to many Italians to be leading to another European war.

timeline	1925	May	National Afterwork Agency (OND) set up
	1926	April	National Balilla Organisation (ONB) formed
	1930		Party urged 'to go resolutely to the people'
	1937		Balilla and Young Fascists form Italian Youth of the Lictors (GIL)

| 1938 | July | Race Manifesto published |
| 1939 | January | The Chamber of Fasces and Corporations set up |

Points to consider

1) What role did the Party play in the fascistisation of Italy?
2) What were the objectives behind Mussolini's educational and youth policy?
3) Does the evidence in this chapter support De Felice's arguments that Mussolini had established a consensus in Italy by the mid 1930s?
4) What role were women intended to play in the Fascist state?
5) Why was the Race Manifesto published in July 1938?

7

THE ITALIAN ECONOMY UNDER MUSSOLINI

MUSSOLINI AS AN ECONOMIST

On the strength of attending a few lectures on economics at Lausanne University Mussolini used to pretend that he had an expert knowledge of the subject. He believed that what counted in economics was will power rather than theory, and thus he often described his economic policy as a series of battles which had to be won. Essentially he wanted to prepare the Italian economy for war and consequently the main thrust of his policy was to build up the heavy industries and encourage agricultural self-sufficiency. In December 1925 he told parliament:

> I consider the Italian nation to be in a permanent state of war . . .
> . . . To live for me means struggle, risk, tenacity . . . not submitting to fate, not even to . . . our so-called deficiency in raw materials.
> <div align="right">(Quoted in <i>Italian Fascism</i>, pp. 97–8)</div>

THE YEARS OF PROSPERITY, 1923–5

Mussolini had an instinctive dislike of capitalism but, particularly in his early years of power, he needed the unqualified support of Italian businessmen and industrialists. Thus he initially went out of his way to create, in Denis Mack Smith's words, a period of 'absolute paradise' for them. The trade unions were destroyed, taxes were lowered and rent controls removed. Mussolini appointed as Minister of Finance an economic liberal, Professor De Stefani, who believed strongly in free enterprise. Not only were telephones and life insurance privatised and the large shipping and steel firm of Ansaldo saved from bankruptcy with generous grants of government money, but taxes on excess war profits were also greatly scaled down. The years 1923–5 were a boom period which was not to be rivalled until the 1950s.

THE BATTLE FOR THE LIRA

However, by the end of 1925 the economy had run into problems. Inflation was rising and the value of the lira was falling steeply against the pound and dollar. The balance of trade was also going sharply into deficit since grain imports had risen by 2.3 million tonnes because of the bad harvest, and industrialists were stockpiling imported raw materials as they wanted to avoid the extra costs resulting from the decline of the lira. Thus to curb inflation and to keep the Italian economy attractive for foreign investment it was important to stabilise the currency. Mussolini rose to the challenge and launched 'the battle for the lira'. For him a strong lira was a matter of national prestige and he impulsively insisted on revaluing it at 90 to the pound, despite the opinion of many businessmen that this was in reality far too high a rate of exchange into sterling.

The revaluation was a turning point in the Italian economy. Italian exports in cars, light engineering and textiles priced themselves out of the world markets. This led to officially imposed wage cuts and the state control of prices and rents. Mussolini, by revaluing so drastically, managed to create a new Fascist economic pattern. The export industries, which depended on world trade, declined, while the steel and chemical industries, which were vital for Mussolini's plans for rearmament, profited from cheaper imported raw materials.

The battle for grain

The 'battle for the lira' was accompanied by the 'battle for grain'. High tariffs were introduced to stop grain imports and, through subsidies, compulsory marketing agencies and the encouragement of new farming techniques, the government did everything it could to increase the amount of wheat grown in Italy. By 1935 the yield had increased by almost two million tonnes, yet this was only achieved at considerable economic cost. In the south olive and citrus fruit trees and vines were destroyed to make way for grain, and valuable export markets, particularly in olive oil, were lost to Spain. Yet 'the battle' did cut the balance of payments deficit and enabled Mussolini to boast that Italy could now feed herself in time of war.

RURALISM

In his Ascension Day speech to the Chamber of Deputies in May 1927 Mussolini launched both 'the battle for births' and the linked policy of ruralism. As discussed in the last chapter, he introduced a wide range of measures to encourage a rise in the birthrate. He was also convinced that its decline could only be halted if the urbanisation of Italy was to be reversed. Like Hitler, Mussolini was convinced that tough and unsophisticated peasants could be turned into good soldiers, while industrial cities produced a degenerate population which married late and had small families. The policy of ruralisation also had the practical advantage of 'exporting' the unemployment problem caused by the high lira back to the villages where it was not so visible.

In the autumn of 1928 Mussolini initiated an 'empty the cities campaign'. The prefects and the police were authorised to stop peasants migrating to the towns to find work, and efforts were made to improve life and the economic infrastructure in the countryside. The 'Mussolini Law' of 1928 made available a large amount of money for land reclamation, road building and aqueducts. Landowners were encouraged to form consortia and given generous grants to improve their own estates. In Tuscany and the Roman Campagna some progress was made. The show piece was the Pontine Marshes which were successfully drained and settled by ex-soldiers. As the marshes were only 55 kilometres from Rome foreign journalists and visitors were frequently taken there to admire the work of the *Duce*. However, only about 250 000 hectares of land were reclaimed and a mere 10 000 landless families settled on it. Overall Mussolini failed to reverse the thrust of modern economic trends. The exodus from the land continued and it was during the 1930s that for the first time less than 50 per cent of the Italian population was employed in farming.

THE GREAT DEPRESSION

By 1930 it was clear that the Italian economy was in recession. Both prices and the value of shares were collapsing. Between 1929 and 1932 car production fell by 50 per cent, steel production declined from 2 122 000 to 1 396 000 tonnes per annum. In the same period unemployment rose from 300 000 to over a million and right across Italy the amount of calories consumed per head fell sharply. The government responded by cutting wages by about 12 per cent, by launching large-scale public works like road building and land drainage schemes and encouraging price fixing and cartel agreements amongst industrialists which stopped cut-throat competition and bankruptcies.

The banking crisis and recovery

The government was also threatened by a major crisis in the banking system. Three of the big banks, *Credito Italiano,* the *Banca Commerciale* and the *Banco di Roma,* were in danger of collapsing because they had loaned large sums of money to firms on the security of their shares which had become valueless as a result of the Depression. To stop a total collapse of both banking and industry the government set up the IMI (*Instituto Mobiliare Italiano*) and then the IRI (Institute for Industrial Reconstruction) to purchase the valueless shares from the banks and then themselves grant long-term loans to industry. Through these new organisations the state acquired an increasingly large stake in the Italian economy. By 1939 it controlled several steel works, shipping lines and shipbuilding companies, as well as the greater part of the Italian electricity and telephone systems. Both the IMI and IRI worked well and helped Italy weather the worst of the Depression more effectively than many other industrial states. The Italian gross national product declined by 5.4 per cent between 1929 and 1933 while the average fall for western Europe as a whole was 7.1 per cent.

Mussolini's propaganda machine inevitably made much of Italy's relative economic success and argued that Fascism through the corporate state (see Chapter 5) had discovered a third way which was an alternative to the inefficiencies of capitalism and the interventionism of communism. He claimed that the IRI was a part of the corporate state, although in reality it was run by a former Liberal politician completely independently of the corporations.

AUTARCHY AND GROWING ECONOMIC DEPENDENCE ON GERMANY

The collapse of Italy's export markets, both as a result of the overvalued lira and then the impact of the Depression, combined to make economic self-sufficiency or autarchy the logical policy for Mussolini to pursue. It involved implementing policies which would reduce imports, control Italy's foreign trade and boost internal production. It also had the important aim of making Italy economically independent in wartime.

Mussolini took the first major step towards autarchy in 1925 when he began the 'battle for grain' with the aim of making Italy self-sufficient in staple foods. Then in the winter of 1934–5 two more key measures aimed at regulating Italy's foreign trade followed. In December no lira could be converted into foreign currency without the permission of the Bank of Italy. In February all imports were temporarily banned from coming into Italy until special bilateral agreements could be negotiated with her trading partners. These measures were concerned to ensure that the cost of paying for the imports in foreign currencies could be covered by the profit made from Italy's exports.

When Italy invaded Ethiopia in 1935, the League of Nations imposed sanctions upon her. Although they were lifted a year later, they inevitably reinforced Mussolini's determination to make Italy as self-sufficient as possible. Considerable ingenuity was devoted to developing *ersatz* or substitute goods. For example, lanital which was made from cheese, replaced wool and rayon proved to be a workable substitute for cotton.

In December 1936 the lira was belatedly devalued by 41 per cent in an attempt to improve Italy's exports. Factories were forced to allocate a larger share of their goods for export and to price them more cheaply than those intended for the home market. Italy's export trade shifted away from western Europe and the United States towards Germany, the Balkan states and the Italian East African empire. By 1939 some 25 per cent of Italy's exports went to her colonial empire and in Europe Germany became her major trading partner. Germany supplied Italy with coal, steel, machine tools and chemicals, while Italy exported to Germany food, wines, silk, cotton and hemp. The Italian and German economies were becoming increasingly enmeshed and reflected the way the Axis agreement was developing into a military alliance (see Chapter 9).

PREPARING FOR WAR 1937-40

During these three years the state's control of the economy greatly increased. The IRI became a permanent institution in 1937, with the power to take over any private company when this was considered necessary in the national interest. A large number of state organisations were set up for organising synthetic raw materials, controlling imports, or running the publicly-owned industries under the IRI. At the end of the 1930s the Italian state directly controlled a greater proportion of private industry than any other European country with the exception of Soviet Russia.

Government expenditure on armaments doubled between 1934 and 1938. Production returned in 1938 to its 1929 level and unemployment in early 1937 officially fell to 700 000, although in reality the figures were probably a good 75 per cent higher. Yet financially this policy was ruinous. Despite an unpopular policy of increased taxes on property, capital and shares, the government deficit rose from 2 billion lira in the year 1934-5 to 28 billion in the year 1938-9. The extra expenditure went mainly on the armament industries, financing the occupation of Ethiopia and military intervention in Spain (see Chapter 9). Autarchy then skewed the Italian economy in an essentially abnormal and unprofitable direction. The aim was no longer to produce what the consumer and the export markets wanted but to prepare for war regardless of the cost.

However, as the military disasters of 1940-3 showed (see Chapter 10), this aim failed. Despite the existence of six economic ministries and large numbers of state agencies supervising various aspects of the economy, there was no effective overall central control. Instead there was a chaos of corporations, quangos and ministries which usually worked in isolation from each other and threatened to strangle the Italian economy in red tape. It was becoming increasingly clear by 1939 that Mussolini's economic policy was not working. No wonder shrewd businessmen began illegally to open bank accounts in Switzerland and transfer their money across the border!

THE CONDITION OF THE PEOPLE

In his first decade of power Mussolini constantly claimed that he did more for the average worker than any other politician in the world. He stressed that it was his main aim to create an equal and prosperous society and abolish the gap between the wealthy and the poor. However in May 1936, just after the conquest of Ethiopia, he dismissed all ideas of prosperity:

> We must rid all our minds of the idea that what we have called the days of prosperity will return. We are probably moving towards the period when humanity will exist on a lower standard of living'
>
> (Quoted in *Italy: a Modern History*, p. 405)

Mussolini was quite right, of course, that the boom years of 1923–5 could not be repeated, yet overall Italy was more prosperous in 1939 than in 1923. On average the gross domestic product increased by 1.2 per cent per year, but this modest increase in prosperity did not filter through equally to all sections of the Italian population.

The industrialists and the great landowners in the north of Italy profited most from Mussolini's regime, but the middle classes also gained stability and protection from socialism and the threat of a red revolution. Their savings, too, were guaranteed from inflation by Mussolini's stubborn insistence on defending the overvalued lira. By doubling the number of public employees, civil servants and teachers from 500 000 to one million, his regime was also able to offer the more educated members of the middle classes secure jobs in the state service.

Mussolini was not so successful in helping the peasantry. Despite his constantly repeated slogan of giving land to the peasants, the low price of food in the inter-war period and the emphasis on growing grain at the expense of fruit, vegetable and wine ensured that in practice the number of small farmers declined from 3.4 million to slightly less than three million in 1931.

The industrial workers fared better under Fascism, although, as we have seen in Chapter 5, their unions were destroyed and the new syndicates were not nearly as effective in defending their interests against the employers. In 1926 they had to work longer hours and between 1928 and 1934 there were wage cuts of about 25 per cent. Yet the workers did benefit from Italy's relatively speedy recovery from the Depression and the syndicates were successful in securing employment and welfare measures for their members. Largely as a result of their efforts in November 1934 a 40-hour week was introduced as a means of spreading the available work amongst a greater number of people, and to compensate those, who had lost eight paid hours of work, family allowances were introduced. Employers also started to agree to Christmas bonuses and holiday pay by the end of the 1930s and to include accident and sickness insurance in pay settlements negotiated with their workers. These benefits, combined with leisure opportunities presented by the National Afterwork Agency (OND), helped allay working-class discontent with the regime. On the whole the workers accepted what was on offer without becoming supporters of Fascism.

For all Mussolini's claims to unify Italy the division between the industrialised north and the backward rural south continued to widen. By the end of the 1930s the northern zone of Italy centring on Milan included some 80 per cent of the industrial and commercial undertakings in the country. In the south, apart from the steel and shipbuilding industries at Naples and Taranto, agriculture was the major industry. Much of the land, as in Sicily for example, was bare and mountainous and uneconomic to farm. Here Fascism's major contribution was to defeat the Mafia, but it failed to underpin this very real achievement with any large-scale economic reforms. Thus the standard of living fell drastically in the south and by 1950, for instance, income per head was only 60 per cent of what it had been in 1924.

The south's problems were made worse when the American government cut down the number of immigrants it was ready to admit into the USA. Thus despite Mussolini's desperate efforts to 'ruralise' Italy wave after wave of southern migrants moved to the northern cities.

Rome grew from under 700 000 in 1921 to 1.4 million in 1940. Milan, Turin and the other large northern cities all expanded as dramatically. The housing situation in Rome was made worse by the wholesale demolition of houses to make way for Mussolini's ambitious plans for building a capital worthy of the new Roman empire. To stop the endless flow of migrants a Commissariat for Internal Migration and Colonisation was set up in 1931 with powers to return people to their own provinces if they had moved illegally, but its efforts were not very effective.

THE CONTRADICTIONS IN MUSSOLINI'S POLICIES

Much of what Mussolini attempted to achieve was contradictory. He wanted to create an autarchic economy, yet Italy was not self-sufficient in raw materials. Essentially he was aiming to turn Italy into a warrior state which, with modern armaments and advanced technology, would found a second Roman empire. For this he needed an advanced industrial base and an expanding but highly educated and skilled workforce of both sexes to build sophisticated weapons. Yet at the same time he wanted to turn the clock back to a pre-industrial period and both create a healthy peasantry which would breed like rabbits to provide future soldiers and confine women to the home. Not surprisingly these reactionary social policies failed: the Italian population did not increase, women continued to work in factories and the drift to the cities gathered momentum. Nor, as the events of 1940–3 were to show (see Chapter 10) did he create an efficient military machine, although heavy industry benefited from his policies and his government, through the IRI, devised a successful way of creating a partnership between private industry and the state which was to serve Italy well in the post-war period.

timeline	1923–5		Boom years
	1925	June	'Battle for grain' launched
	1926	August	'Battle for the lira' begins
	1929–33		Impact of the Great Depression
	1934–8		Expenditure on armaments doubled

Points to consider

1) How effectively did Mussolini prepare the Italian economy for war?
2) 'The Italian people were compensated for their loss of political freedom by an increase in their economic prosperity.' Discuss.

8

FOREIGN POLICY AND EMPIRE, 1922–36

THE BASIC PROBLEM OF ITALIAN FOREIGN POLICY

Essentially Fascism glorified war and exalted the nation state. It believed too, that, eventually the new virile Italy would replace the 'decadent' British and French as rulers of a vast Mediterranean and African empire, yet when Mussolini took over the Foreign Ministry in October 1922 there was no sudden radical change in Italian foreign policy, although his style of diplomacy was very different from the career diplomats. His own programme was broadly in harmony with the traditional aims of the Italian Foreign Office. Like his officials, and indeed most Italians, he believed that the Allies had cheated Italy of her just rewards in the peace treaties of 1919 and had 'mutilated' her victory. Although Italy gained south Tyrol and the security of the Brenner frontier together with the Istrian peninsula and the important city of Trieste, she failed to acquire either Fiume or the Dalmatian coastline, which she had been promised by the Treaty of London in 1915. Neither did she make any significant annexations when the Turkish and German colonial empires were redistributed between the victorious powers. As Italy lacked both the economic and military resources of a great power, Mussolini's only hope of implementing his ambitious programme was to win the backing of strong allies or or else skilfully to exploit international tensions and rivalries to extract valuable concessions, as the Salandra Cabinet did in 1915 through the Treaty of London.

In the course of 1922–3 the weakness of Italy's position became all too clear to Mussolini. First, he failed to gain any substantial concessions in Africa or the Middle East from Britain and France when they negotiated a new peace treaty with Mustapha Kemal at the Lausanne Conference after his successful resistance had defeated attempts to impose the punitive Treaty of Sèvres on Turkey. Then, secondly, he was also unsuccessful in exploiting in the interests of Italy the international crisis caused by the French occupation of the Ruhr in January 1923. He veered from trying to mediate between France and Britain, who opposed the occupation, to proposing at one point a potentially anti-British trading bloc composed of the main Continental states. Not surprisingly, London and Paris both distrusted him and he remained a marginal player on the European stage.

The Corfu incident

The reality behind Fascist rhetoric was briefly revealed, however, during the Corfu incident. In August 1923 an Italian general and his staff, who were busy mapping out for an international inter-Allied Commission the new Greek–Albanian frontier, were murdered on Greek territory. Mussolini immediately sent an ultimatum to the Greek government insisting on compensation of 50 million lira, which it refused. He then seized the chance to occupy Corfu, a strategically important island guarding the southern entrance to the Adriatic. When Greece appealed to the League of Nations, Mussolini not only rejected the League's intervention but began to build a military base on the island. In the end, as a compromise, the British and French agreed that the question of compensation should be settled independently of the League but insisted that Italian forces should withdraw immediately from the island. The incident was celebrated by the Fascist press as a great success for Mussolini: not only had the League been defied, but the occupation of the island was the first real example of a Fascist foreign policy. Yet in reality it was a diplomatic defeat for Mussolini. Far from securing the important island base of Corfu he had been forced to withdraw by Anglo–French pressure.

ITALY AND THE GREAT POWERS, 1924–30

The Corfu incident gave Mussolini the reputation of being a dangerous firebrand, yet the seemingly impregnable position of Britain and

France in the Mediterranean and Europe forced him into adopting a more conventional foreign policy. He could not run the risk of permanantly isolating Italy in Europe. Thus when Britain, France, Belgium and Germany began to negotiate the Locarno pact, Mussolini at first refused to participate, but then, fearing the consequences of being left out, joined Britain as one of the guarantors of the demilitarised Rhineland and the Franco–German frontiers.

Locarno was an important agreement which marked the end of the immediate post-war period. Germany was no longer isolated and was accepted as an equal by Britain and France. Up to 1925 Italy's only chance of modifying the peace settlement had been to co-operate closely with the Anglo–French *Entente*. Now with Germany's return to the ranks of the great powers there was more freedom for Mussolini to play off one state against another. For the next five years it was British friendship that enabled Mussolini to gain concessions in North Africa and pursue his ambitions in the Balkans despite French suspicions. Austen Chamberlain, the British Foreign Secretary, had been pleased by Anglo–Italian cooperation at Locarno and personally admired the *Duce*. At the end of 1925 he agreed that Italy should take over Jarabub on the Libyan–Egyptian border and he also recognised the legitimacy of Italy's claim to influence over a large part of Ethiopia. This did not, of course prevent Mussolini from encouraging anti-British movements in Egypt and elsewhere in the Arab world.

Relations with France were not so friendly. The French were reluctant to take Italy seriously as a great power. Also the constant stream of Fascist propaganda stressing the need to revise the peace treaties and to pursue an active foreign policy in the Balkans clashed with France's determination to defend the post-war settlement and to negotiate a series of pacts with the Balkan states. Good relations were also made more difficult by the election of a left-wing government in Paris in 1924 and, after Matteotti's murder, by the constantly growing number of Italian refugees who sought refuge in France. Mussolini attempted to bring pressure to bear on France by pretending to draw closer to Germany. Thus the importance of the German–Italian arbitration treaty of 1926, which was nothing more than a standard statement of goodwill between two powers, was greatly exaggerated by the Fascist press. Mussolini's own monthly periodical, *Gerarchia*, for instance, trumpeted

... the brotherhood of arms between Italy and France is ... now
lost ... Italy has now returned to her traditional ties with Germany
on the Continent and with England in the Mediterranean.

(Quoted in C. J. Lowe and F. Marzari, *Italian Foreign Policy,
1870–1940*, Routledge, 1975, p. 213)

MUSSOLINI'S POLICY IN THE BALKANS

Mussolini hoped to eliminate French influence from the Balkans and
create there a series of client states which would look to Rome rather
than Paris. After the failure of gun boat diplomacy on Corfu, he tried a
more conciliatory policy. In early 1924 he peacefully acquired Fiume
from Yugoslavia through a treaty which pledged mutual 'support and
cordial collaboration' and then negotiated a similar agreement with
Czechoslovakia. He also cultivated close contacts with what his
government stressed was 'Latin Romania'. In 1926, however, his policy
again became more aggressive when he began planning to undermine
the Yugoslav state. At times he considered launching 20 divisions across
the frontier, but in the end he settled on the more low-key policy of
subsidising Macedonian and Croat separatist movements. He also
supported the revisionist claims of Hungary against Yugoslavia and
smuggled weapons over the frontier to help her illegally evade the
restrictions imposed upon her by the Treaty of Trianon.

The main centre of Italian influence in the Balkans lay in Albania.
Italy had occupied Albania in the First World War, but had then been
forced out by a nationalist rebellion in 1920. By 1926 Mussolini had re-
established Italian influence there by backing the claims to power of a
local chieftain, Ahmed Zog, and by investing heavily in the economy.
Italian officers were also sent over to train the Albanian army in the
expectation of war against Yugoslavia. By 1928 Albania was in fact, even
if not legally so, an Italian colony. Plans were already being drawn up
for settling Italian peasants in the more fertile regions and driving the
native Albanian population out into the more mountainous regions.
The Italian colonisation of Albania was seen by Mussolini as 'the first
stage in our Imperial journey'.

ITALIAN COLONIAL POLICY IN THE 1920s

Before 1914 Mussolini had been violently opposed to colonisation but his views had changed during the war and once in power he was convinced that Fascism had a mission to create a great empire. In 1922 Italy possessed an assortment of territories, some of which were still not properly controlled from Rome: the Dodecanese Islands, Libya, Somalia and Eritrea. Mussolini often talked of sending millions of Italians to settle in the colonies and of creating large new markets for Italian industry. In fact the colonies proved to be an expensive drain on Italian resources and only some 50 000 Italians ever made their home there.

During the 1920s considerable progress was made in consolidating Italy's grip on her existing territories. In Somalia the northern sultanates which in practice had governed themselves, became more firmly subjugated to Italian colonial rule after a two-year military campaign. Similarly in Libya, Mussolini ignored an agreement negotiated in 1919 which allowed Tripoli and Cyrenaica to have their own assemblies and ordered the new governor, Giuseppi Volpi, to make Italian administration a reality. A protracted and brutal war was waged against the weak local forces, which managed to hold out until 1932.

Whilst consolidating his grip on Italy's existing colonies Mussolini also pursued his main objective of absorbing Ethiopia, which had long been seen in Rome as a legitimate area for Italian influence. A treaty of friendship was signed with Haile Selassi, the Emperor of Ethiopia, in 1928, which Mussolini hoped would lead to Ethiopia becoming an Italian satellite, but by signing similar agreements with other powers the Emperor was cleverly able to avoid that fate. From 1929 onwards Italian troops began to exploit the absence of a clearly marked frontier to occupy illegally areas actually inside Ethiopia. Plans were also drawn up for an eventual full-scale invasion of the country.

THE IMPACT OF THE DEPRESSION AND THE RISE OF HITLER

The Great Depression has been called by one historian, Robert Bryce, the 'third global catastrophe of the century'. It destroyed the new post-war economic system dominated by Washington and London into which Italy was locked. America retreated into isolation and tried to revive her economy behind high tariff walls, while Britain and France concentrated on building up trade with their empires. It consequently became easier for Mussolini to pursue his own independent foreign policy and to consolidate the Italian empire in Africa by annexing Ethiopia.

A further consequence of the Depression was the rise to power of Hitler and the re-emergence of an aggressive and revisionist Germany to challenge the Anglo–French domination of Europe. At first it seemed as if Italy would now at last be able to exploit this situation and play the two sides off against each other and gain important concessions as she did in 1915. Mussolini welcomed Hitler's success and immediately claimed that Germany was following Italy's example. Hitler was duly showered with advice about how to run Germany and build a corporate state. Hitler in his turn sent his 'admiration and homage' to Mussolini, and expressed his wish for an alliance with Italy. One major area of disagreement between the two dictators was, however, foreshadowed when Hitler made clear that Germany would ultimately absorb Austria. The prospect of once more having a great power on her northern frontier threatened to undo Italy's main gain from the peace treaties of 1919. Not surprisingly the question of Austria was to be a disruptive factor in German–Italian relations for the next three years.

The four-power pact

Initially Mussolini hoped that he would be able to hold the balance between France and Germany. In March 1933 he proposed setting up a four-power directory consisting of Britain, France, Germany and Italy, which would revise the peace treaties, arrange for Germany to re-arm up to the level of the western powers and create a new framework for cooperation over both European and colonial problems. In all these negotiations Mussolini optimistically hoped that there would be many chances for Italy to play off France against Germany and in the process increase both her influence and her power. In practice, as a result of the objections of the other three powers, only a very watered down and almost meaningless version of the Pact was signed in July. Nevertheless in Italy it was welcomed by the Fascist press as yet another example of

Mussolini is depicted in December 1936 by the Egyptian cartoonist, 'Kem', as the she-wolf from Rome's Capitoline Hill suckling Europe's 'infant' Fascists: (L. to R.) Hitler, Kemal Attaturk, Metaxas of Greece, General Franco with, far right, Mosley waiting his turn.

Mussolini's genius in making Italy the centre of Europe. In December Hitler's decision to withdraw from the League of Nations and to start to re-arm brought an abrupt end to the Pact.

GERMANY AND THE AUSTRIAN PROBLEM

Mussolini had intervened actively in Austrian politics since 1927 when he had begun to support with money and arms the Austrian *Heimwehr*, a coalition of extreme right-wing and patriotic volunteer groups which had been set up to protect Austria's new frontiers in 1919. He made it very clear that he would not support an *Anschluss* or union between Austria and Germany, but he hoped the *Heimwehr* would be able to create a Fascist and Catholic Austria that would look south to Rome. Their leader, Starhemberg, readily agreed with him. His influence in Austria was further strengthened when Dollfuss, the Austrian Chancellor, formed a coalition with the *Heimwehr* in 1932. A few months later in February 1933 Starhemberg signed an agreement in Rome which firmly rejected any possibility of an *Anschluss*.

Hitler's seizure of power was a serious threat to Italian influence in Austria. As an Austrian Hitler was determined that this small country should eventually form part of Germany, but in 1933 Germany was too weak to defy the peace treaties and simply move her troops over the frontier. Instead Hitler employed methods similar to those used by Mussolini. He hoped to undermine an independent Austria by demanding a prominent place in the government for the Austrian National Socialists. When Dollfuss rejected this, Hitler launched violent attacks on him both in the press and on the radio and also threatened Austria's tourist trade by imposing a heavy tax on Germans who had visited the country. Inevitably Dollfuss turned to Mussolini for help. Mussolini, of course, had no desire for a conflict with Germany. He wanted to continue to balance between Berlin, Paris and London, while strengthening Italy's position in Austria and the Balkans. Thus when he met Dollfuss at Rimini in August 1933 he advised him to seek a settlement with Hitler, but a settlement which was not to be seen as a prelude to an *Anschluss*. Indeed, to stop that from happening both statesmen agreed that if Germany attempted to tighten her grip on Austria, Italy would move 5000 troops up to the German frontier.

Gradually, however, German pressure on Austria forced Mussolini to come out as the defender of the status quo in the Balkans. In March 1934 he signed the Rome Protocols, with Austria and Hungary, which provided for tripartite consultations should any of the three powers call for them. In June Hitler met Mussolini at Venice and attempted unsuccessfully to come to an agreement with him over the future of Austria. The assassination of Dollfuss and the attempt in July by the Austrian Nazis to seize power in Vienna ended Mussolini's efforts to balance between Berlin, London and Paris. He rushed four Italian divisions up to the Brenner frontier and persuaded the *Heimwehr* to crush the Nazis in Vienna. A direct consequence of this attempted coup was an increase in cooperation between Italy and France which resulted in the Rome Agreements of January 1935. Long-standing problems in Tunisia were resolved, Italy was allowed to extend the frontiers of Libya southwards and both countries agreed to consultations if Germany broke any of the limitations imposed upon her by the Treaty of Versailles. Thus when Hitler openly ignored the disarmament clauses of the Treaty by introducing conscription in March, Mussolini together with the French and British prime ministers met a month later at Stresa and agreed to maintain the peace treaties of 1919–20 and to oppose any attempt to change them by force. A few months later the Italian General Staff met their French counterparts and began to draw up plans for joint operations against Germany on the Rhine and the Brenner should war break out.

It seemed as if Mussolini was at last giving up his policy of balancing between Germany and France, but this did not mean that Italy had become a 'satisfied power' and Mussolini an elder statesman. On the contrary he hoped to strike a bargain with both Britain and France that in return for his support in Europe they would tolerate Italian control of Ethiopia.

THE ETHIOPIAN WAR

Historians do not agree on the real causes of the Ethiopian war. Some see it more as an anachronistic colonial war waged at a time when the re-emergence of a strong Germany had lead to a balance of power in Europe. Others stress that it was a response to the Depression and a way out of the internal political and economic crisis in Italy. It is true that Italian Nationalists had long urged the government to occupy Ethiopia and revenge Adowa. There was a marked continuity in Italy's foreign policy stretching back to the turn of the century. In some ways the Depression provided Mussolini with compelling arguments for the occupation. Ethiopia was believed to be rich in raw materials and seen as a future market for Italian industry. Mussolini constantly claimed that Italy was a 'proletarian' or poor nation fighting to grab a greater share of colonies and raw materials at the expense of the plutocratic or wealthy powers, Britain and France. Yet the war was not caused just by economic factors. As discussed in Chapter 7, there was no political crisis in Italy during the Depression and the economy was in better shape than in many other countries. There was another dimension to the war; some historians argue that it was a 'Fascist war' which was to a great extent fought to mobilise the Italian population and accustom it to the coming era of perpetual war. If victorious it would enable Mussolini to begin to outflank the powerful conservative forces in industry, the civil service and the army, and accelerate the 'fascistisation' of Italian society.

In 1932 Mussolini took back the running of the Italian Foreign Office from Dino Grandi, to whom it had been given in 1929 and preparations for war were speeded up. It was planned to provoke Ethiopia into taking action against Italy by a carefully stage-managed incident, which would, of course, give Italy an excuse for war and satisfy Britain and France that she was the injured party.

The Wal-Wal incident

In 1930 the Italians occupied the important watering hole of Wal-Wal. some 50 miles inside Ethiopian territory. Four years later in 1934 an Anglo–Ethiopian boundary commission started to mark out the far-from-clear frontier between British Somaliland and Ethiopia. In November protected by some 600 Ethiopian soldiers, it arrived at Wal-Wal where there was a small Italian garrison of colonial troops. A scuffle broke out between the soldiers on both sides. The British officials quickly withdrew, but then on 5 December fighting started between the Italians and Ethiopians in which about 150 men were killed and the Ethiopians were forced to retreat. This incident brought matters to a head. Haile Selassi seized the chance to challenge Italy's illegal occupation by appealing to the League of Nations. Mussolini was determined to insist on Italy's claim and go to war, once his military preparations were complete. On 30 December 1934 in a secret memorandum for the Italian Foreign Office he wrote:

> It is imperative that the problem be resolved as soon as possible, as soon as our military preparations will give us the certainty of victory . . . the objective can be no other than the destruction of the Abyssinian [sic] armed forces and the total conquest of Ethiopia. The Empire cannot be made any other way.
>
> (Quoted in *Italian Foreign Policy*, p. 254)

Diplomatic preparations

From January to October 1935 Mussolini attempted to gain Anglo–French agreement for his plans to annex Ethiopia. He had little difficulty with the French, who were quite ready to write off Ethiopia in return for Italian assistance in Europe against Germany. At first the British, too, seemed quite willing to give Mussolini a free hand. They dropped their own plans for giving the Emperor the port of Zeila in British Somaliland in exchange for the control of the grazing land around Wal-Wal, and, together with France, advised him to abandon his appeal to the League in favour of arbitration. After the Stresa meeting Mussolini was reasonably convinced in the words of Lowe and Marzari, that 'if London would not close both eyes as Paris had done, it would close at least one'. He was also aware from the work of a spy within the British embassy in Rome that the British had no real interests in the heartland of Ethiopia.

Yet increasingly over the summer British opposition to an Italian invasion of that country stiffened. This was partly due to public opinion and the imminence of a General Election. In an unofficial peace ballot in Britain organised by the League of Nations Union in June 1935 10 out of 11 million replies backed the use of economic sanctions by the League in a case of aggression. Britain also appreciated the advantages of supporting the system of collective security through the League, which gave protection to her own vulnerable empire. Thus the British now supported by the French, who could not afford a break with London, tried hard to find compromise solutions that involved giving

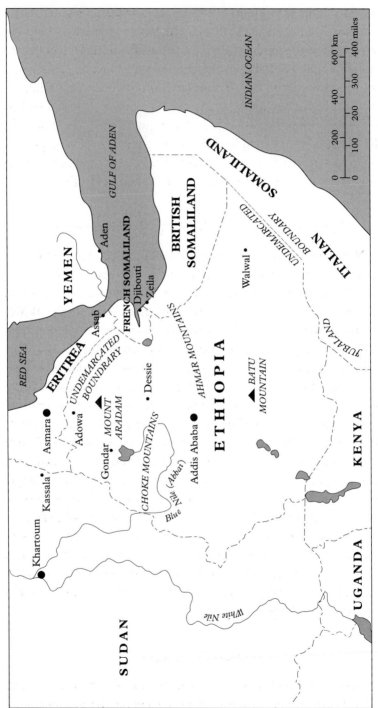

Ethiopia in 1935

Italy a preponderant influence in Ethiopia without totally destroying that country's independence. In June, for instance, Britain offered to cede to Ethiopia the port of Zeila provided the Emperor then both gave the Ogaden region to Italy and also granted her economic concessions. This, as indeed were all the other offers, was rejected by Mussolini.

Meanwhile Mussolini continued to build up his forces in Italian East Africa and by September 1935 he had an army of nearly a quarter of a million men there. He had become so committed to the conquest of Ethiopia that he could not afford to retreat without a disastrous blow to his prestige. On 3 October he ordered the invasion to begin.

The League's reaction and the Hoare–Laval plan

On 7 November the Council of the League of Nations declared Italy to have violated Article XII of the Covenant, which bound members to submit disputes to arbitration, and on 18 November a series of economic sanctions gradually came into effect. At first the British government, which was in the middle of its own election campaign, thought that support for the League and a tough line towards Italy would please the electorate. However once the election was won, French desire for a rapid agreement and the deep reluctance of the British Admiralty to risk war against Italy in the Mediterranean ensured that the British, too, were willing to seek a compromise. Consequently in December the British Foreign Secretary, Hoare, and the French Premier, Laval, drew up a plan very similar to the one already suggested by Britain in June. Considerable areas of northern and eastern Ethiopia were to be ceded to Italy while Italy would be given exclusive economic influence in a huge zone in the south of the country. On 18 December Mussolini and the Fascist Grand Council actually accepted the plan 'as a possible basis for discussion'. However, a few days earlier the plan had been leaked to the French press and an explosion of rage amongst supporters of the League forced first Hoare's and then Laval's resignations, and the plan was dropped.

Mussolini's triumph?

By the end of December the Ethiopian counter-attack on the Italian forces at Mount Aradam had been defeated and the way was open for a rapid Italian advance. Mussolini ordered the Italian army to employ every means, including the use of poison gas, to destroy the enemy, and on 5 May 1936 General Badoglio entered Addis Ababa. Mussolini claimed that Italy had 'won the greatest colonial war known to history' and three days later proclaimed the existence of the Italian Empire.

Renzo de Felice has called the war Mussolini's political masterpiece. He had defied the League of Nations and defeated Britain diplomatically. The League's ineffective policy of sanctions, which excluded oil, ensured that Britain and France gained the worst of both worlds. They failed to stop the war and also succeeded in uniting Italian public opinion around Mussolini. Most historians would agree with Philip Morgan that the war 'marked the high point of support and consent for the Fascist regime'. One particularly successful part of the propaganda campaign was the 'day of faith' on 18 December 1935 when thousands of Italians, including the royal family, handed over their gold wedding rings to the state.

However the triumph was short lived. The next five years were to show that Ethiopia was an expensive drain on Italy's financial resources. Although the facts were hidden from the Italians, the war did not properly end in May 1936. In reality right up to 1941, despite savage reprisals which also involved attempts to liquidate the state's western-educated young intellectuals, only a relatively small area of Ethiopia was ever under Italian control and unrest spread across the borders to Eritrea. This was to make Mussolini's declaration of 'victory' look more like 'a propaganda stunt' (Mack Smith) than an expression of reality.

HITLER BENEFITS

The unravelling of the Franco–Italian Entente and of the Stresa Front in the winter of 1935–6 inevitably led to an improvement in relations between Germany and Italy. Once the League of Nations started on its policy of sanctions, Italy became increasingly dependent on imported coal from Germany. It was, too, very much in Hitler's interests that the war in Ethiopia should continue and not be ended by a compromise between Italy, France and Britain which would enable those three powers to work together again.

In December the Germans began to plan the military re-occupation of the Rhineland, which according to the Treaty of Versailles was to remain a demilitarised zone. In February 1936 Mussolini made it quite clear that, even though Italy was one of the guarantors of demilitarisation under the Locarno Pact, he would not protest if Germany re-occupied the Rhineland. Indeed, such a move would take the pressure off Italy and shift attention away from Ethiopia back to Germany. As sanctions continued up to July 1936, there was no immediate chance at the 'official' end of the Ethiopian war of restoring the Stresa Front and German–Italian relations consequently continued to improve. Mussolini now had to be more flexible over Austria. While he was still opposed to a formal *Anschluss*, he urged the Austrians to come to terms with the Germans and negotiate a general settlement with them. They had little option but to take his advice. On 11 July an agreement was signed whereby Austria retained her independence but harmonised her foreign policy with Germany's. The agreement was a considerable success for Hitler and marked the beginning of the end of Italy's influence in Austria. It was becoming obvious that Mussolini had gained an empire at the cost of his position in central Europe.

a note on . . .

AUSTRIA

In November 1918 the Austro-Hungarian Empire collapsed. The Czechs declared an independent republic and the Southern Slavs broke away to form with Serbia what was to become the Yugoslav state. The Treaty of St Germain set up a new and much reduced Austrian state of a population of some six million. Both the treaties of St Germain and Versailles specifically vetoed any union (*Anschluss*) between Austria and Germany as France did not want to strengthen Germany. Austria was a small, impoverished and unstable state with a large mainly socialist population in Vienna, its capital city. Austrian politics were polarised between the Socialists and the *Heimwehr*. The Austrian Socialists had run the country up to 1920 and been responsible for drafting the new constitution. Increasingly the *Heimwehr* came to see this as an instrument for imposing socialism on Austria and began to look instead towards Fascism and the corporate state as a rival model. In 1931 in the midst of the Great Depression, however, both sides saw the advantage of a customs union with Germany. It would at least create markets for Austrian goods at a time when the Balkan states were putting up tariff barriers against them, but this was stopped by the French with the backing of the Italians on the grounds that it would lead to an eventual *Anschluss*.

ETHIOPIA, 1867–1930

Ethiopia was far from a unified state. It was made up of several self-governing and often feuding kingdoms. By the end of the nineteenth century this old-fashioned and divided state seemed to be about to fall victim to European colonisation. In 1896 with the support of the British the Italians sent in an expeditionary force, but this was annihilated at Adowa with the loss of nearly 6000 men. This victory under Emperor Menelik temporarily stabilised the kingdom and in 1906 Britain, France and Italy signed an agreement to maintain its independence. When Menelik died in 1913 there was another period of acute instability and near civil war until Ras Tafari, the son of the man whom Menelik had originally chosen as his successor, was crowned Emperor Haile Selassie in 1930. Much to Mussolini's alarm he was a moderniser who wanted to bring his country into the twentieth century.

timeline	1923	August	The Corfu incident
	1925	October	The Locarno Conference
	1933	January	Hitler comes to power
	1934	August	Dollfuss murdered
	1935	January	Rome Agreements
		April	Stresa Agreements
		October	Start of Ethiopian War
	1936	March	Rhineland re-militarised

Points to consider

1) To what extent did Mussolini pursue a consistent foreign policy between 1922–36?
2) Why was the Nazi regime a threat to Italian interests in Europe and how did Mussolini seek to defend them?
3) 'If Mussolini had known that he would lose the support of Britain and France he would never have started the Ethiopian War'. Discuss.

9

MUSSOLINI AND HITLER, JULY 1936–JUNE 1940

HISTORIANS AND MUSSOLINI'S FOREIGN POLICY

Historians disagree as to whether there was an inevitable sequence of events leading from the Ethiopian War to the Pact of Steel, the Italian–German alliance of May 1939. De Felice, for instance, was convinced that Mussolini was still trying to exploit Britain's fear of Germany to extract further colonial concessions from her. He was, so the argument runs, continuing to follow a ' "pendulum policy" – the oscillation between Germany and England – the so-called policy of the "determinant weight" ' (Quoted in *The Historical Journal*, **36(1)**, 1993, p. 201). Other historians like Philip Morgan, Felix Gilbert and Manfred Funke believe that the announcement of the Axis Agreement in October marked a fundamental turning point in Italian foreign policy, comparable in importance to May 1915, and that Mussolini decided to align Italy from that point on with Germany rather than with the western powers.

THE SPANISH CIVIL WAR

The Spanish Civil War, which broke out in July 1936 with a Nationalist revolt led by the army against the Republican government, deepened the rift between Italy and Britain and France, and aligned Mussolini more firmly with Germany. When the rebels were at first defeated in a number of cities by armed workers, both sides appealed to the international community for help. The Nationalists led by General Franco approached Italy and Germany, while the Republicans looked in vain to Britain and France and then more successfully to Soviet Russia. Both Hitler and Mussolini, agreed to help Franco with aircraft, arms, munitions and troops. Mussolini was convinced that a right-wing semi-Fascist government in Spain led by General Franco would be a useful ally in the Mediterranean against the British and French. Franco might also grant Italy economic privileges in Spain and a naval base on the Balearic Islands. On the other hand, Mussolini feared that the French Socialist government under Leon Blum would intervene to help the Republicans. Triumphant after his victory in Ethiopia, he welcomed intervention as a means for further toughening up the Italian character. The Italians had, as he said, to 'be kept up to the mark by kicks on their shins'!

Mussolini assumed that the Civil War would quickly be over, but it dragged on until the spring of 1939. After the defeat of Italian troops at Guadalajara in March 1937, the very prestige of the regime seemed at stake and consequently Mussolini could not afford to withdraw until Franco was victorious. The struggle became increasingly ideological. It aligned Italy with Nazi Germany in a struggle against the Republicans who were supplied with advisers and equipment by Soviet Russia. London and Paris, in an effort to stop the war from spreading, proposed a non-intervention agreement, which was signed by both Germany and Italy. In practice, however, both Hitler and Mussolini ignored the agreement and attacks by Italian submarines on Russian, British and French shipping in the Mediterranean caused further deterioration in relations between the western democracies and Rome.

THE ROME–BERLIN AXIS

Symbolic of the new closeness in Italian–German relations was the visit to Germany in October 1936 of Mussolini's son-in-law, Ciano, the Italian Foreign Minister. After wide-ranging talks with Hitler and Neurath, his opposite number in Germany, the October Protocols were signed. Italy conceded German predominance in Austria, while Germany recognised the Italian empire in East Africa. Both governments agreed on the danger of Communism and the need to keep a careful watch on alleged British plans for encirclement. There was also to be close cooperation between the two powers in Spain.

On Sunday 1 November Mussolini, in a speech in Milan, explained the importance of the the October Protocols to his fellow Italians:

> The Berlin conversations have resulted in an understanding between our two countries over certain problems which have been particularly acute. But these understandings which have been sanctioned in fitting and duly signed agreements, this Berlin–Rome line, is not a diaphragm but rather an axis around which can revolve all those European states with a will to collaboration and peace.
>
> (Quoted in E. Wiskemann, *The Rome–Berlin Axis*, Fontana, 1966, p. 92)

The Axis was not a formal treaty and Mussolini was by no means committed to a German alliance. Some historians, like De Felice and D. C. Watt see it as 'the blackmailer's card', which Mussolini hoped would extract further concessions from Britain and France. If this was so, it was not very successful. In a series of low-key negotiations with Britain in 1937 and 1938, he achieved little more than British recognition of the Italian conquest of Ethiopia.

Mussolini's visit to Berlin, September 1937

A year later the Axis was further strengthened when Hitler invited Mussolini to Germany. Lowe and Marzari have called this visit 'one of the most crucial events of the inter-war period'. After witnessing army manoeuvres, inspecting Krupp's armament factories in Essen and addressing a mass meeting in Berlin (which was interrupted by a thunderstorm and faulty loud speakers), Mussolini seemed more convinced than ever that Nazism was an invincible force in Europe and that Italy had no choice but to ally herself with it. He thus distanced himself further from Britain and France. On 6 November he joined Germany and Japan in the Anti-Comintern Pact, an agreement of more symbolic than practical importance aimed at the Communist International, and a month later left the League of Nations. He also made it quite clear to Ribbentrop, the German Foreign Minister, that

Italy's interest in Austrian affairs was 'no longer as lively as it was some years ago, for one thing because of Italy's imperialist development, which was now concentrating her interest in the Mediterranean and the Colonies'. He then went on to stress that the best solution was 'to let events take their natural course . . . France knows that if a crisis should arise in Austria, Italy would do nothing'. Nevertheless both Ciano and Mussolini still hoped that such a crisis might be long delayed. A few months earlier Mussolini had advised Schuschnigg, the Austrian Chancellor, to organise Austria's domestic affairs in such a way that Hitler would have no excuse to intervene.

The Anschluss

Mussolini was therefore far from pleased when Schuschnigg went to Berlin in February 1938 and was presented by Hitler with a ten-point ultimatum, which within a month was to lead to the *Anschluss*. Italy's weakness was underlined by the fact that neither Schuschnigg nor Hitler bothered to contact Rome. In desperation Ciano turned to Britain in an effort to speed up the Anglo–Italian negotiations which had been proceeding only very slowly over the previous six months, in the hope that this might just persuade Hitler to be more cautious in his approach to Austria. However, when Schuschnigg attempted to renounce the ultimatum by asking his countrymen to vote in a referendum which he planned to hold on Sunday 14 March for a 'free and German, independent and social, Christian and united Austria', Mussolini was powerless to back him and, on hearing from Hitler's special messenger, the Prince of Hess, on 12 March that German troops were about to occupy Austria, Mussolini told Hitler that 'Italy is following events with absolute calm'.

Italy had now lost the advantage she had gained at St Germain. Once again she had a great power on the Brenner frontier, whose influence would be increasingly felt in the Balkans. Mussolini was paying the price for his break with Britain and France in 1935. A few days after the *Anschluss* he attempted to rationalise Italy's impotence by arguing 'that when an event is fated to take place, it's better it takes place with you rather than despite of, or worse still, against you'.

MUSSOLINI'S POLICY TOWARDS BRITAIN AND FRANCE

Clearly one way for Mussolini to escape from the German orbit was to negotiate agreements with Britain and France and try to return to Italy's traditional policy of 'equidistance' between the western powers and Berlin. At times he appeared to explore this option but essentially his territorial demands were so great that he could only achieve them with German backing. He aimed not so much to hold the balance between the western powers and Germany as to use German power to frighten them into making major concessions. To do this effectively he had to gravitate ever more closely towards Germany.

In February 1939 he explained to the Fascist Grand Council what his foreign policy aims were:

> Italy has in fact no free access to the oceans; Italy is really a prisoner in the Mediterranean and the more populous and powerful she becomes, the more she will suffer from her imprisonment.
>
> The bars of the prison are Corsica, Tunisia, Malta and Cyprus: its sentinels Gibraltar and Suez . . .
>
> The tasks of Italian policy which could not and does not have European territorial aims, save Albania, is in the first place to break the prison bars. . . .
>
> We are faced with the opposition of Britain and France. To brave the solution of such problems without having first secured our rear on the continent would have been absurd. The Rome–Berlin Axis thus answers a fundamental necessity. The same applies to our conduct in the Spanish Civil War.
>
> (Quoted in *Italian Foreign Policy*, p. 316)

THE SUDETEN CRISIS

Ultimately Italian ambitions in the Mediterranean could only be achieved through war, but Mussolini realised that Italy would not be ready for war until at least 1941–2. In the meantime it was essential to restrain Hitler from triggering a premature conflict in central Europe. Consequently when it looked in September 1938 as if Hitler was about to plunge Europe into war over his demands for the immediate annexation of the Sudetenland, which had been given by the Treaty of St Germain to Czechoslavakia in 1919, Mussolini quickly responded to appeals from Chamberlain, the British Prime Minister, to mediate. He proposed to Hitler that a four-power conference should meet at Munich on 29 September to work out a compromise. Mussolini skilfully achieved this by persuading Chamberlain and Daladier, the French Premier, to accept Hitler's minimum demands. These involved delaying the occupation from 1 until 10 October and allowing an international commission to map the new boundary line between German Sudetenland and Czechoslovakia.

There is no doubt that the Munich agreement was a considerable diplomatic success for Mussolini and ironically he was praised all over the world as the man who had saved the peace. Mussolini had effectively stopped Hitler plunging Europe into war before he judged Italy to be ready for it.

NEGOTIATIONS FOR A MILITARY ALLIANCE WITH GERMANY

Throughout the summer of 1938 Hitler had been pressing to turn the Axis into a proper alliance. In November the pressure was renewed, but the Italian government was not ready to commit itself after its diplomatic triumph at Munich. Ciano strongly advised that Italy should maintain close contacts with Britain and France:

> We must keep both doors open. An alliance would now close, perhaps forever, one of the two, and that not the less important. The *Duce* also seems to think so.
>
> (Quoted in *Italian Foreign Policy*, p. 319)

Here indeed is some evidence of Italy's traditional policy of 'equidistance' but it did not last for long. When Britain and France began discussions on a military alliance in December, Mussolini decided in principle to negotiate a full military alliance with Germany, although detailed talks did not begin until the following April. Yet he still had no intention of fighting France and Britain for several years. A German alliance was therefore intended to be more an instrument of diplomatic pressure than a prelude to war. Mussolini hoped it would, for instance, enable him to occupy Albania without fear of Anglo–French retaliation.

The occupation of Albania

Mussolini's calculations were indeed proved correct. When Italian troops invaded Albania on 7 April 1939 he enjoyed the support of Berlin, but paradoxically the occupation was a defensive act and in many ways anti-German. The Nazi occupation of Prague on 15 March had at one go destroyed the Munich settlement, of which Mussolini had been the proud architect, and significantly strengthened Germany's position in south-eastern Europe. Not surprisingly therefore the Italian embassies in London and Paris were instructed

> If our military occupation of Albania takes place . . . to spread the information that the Italian action is designed to block further German expansion in the Balkans.
>
> (Quoted in *Italian Foreign Policy*, p. 328)

This message did little to reassure London and Paris and the occupation led rapidly to the Anglo–French guarantees of Greece and Romania.

The Pact of Steel

The increasingly close collaboration between Britain and France speeded up the signature of the Italian–German alliance, or Pact of Steel, as Mussolini called it on 22 May 1939. Mussolini believed that he had gained two important advantages: an alliance with the strongest power in Europe and several years of peace in which he could build up his forces and exploit the political advantages of his alliance with Germany to extract concessions from Britain and France in the Mediterranean and the Balkans. The Treaty, however, committed both powers to assist each other in the event of war whenever it might break out. Although during the negotiations Mussolini and Ciano had constantly stressed that Italy would not be ready for war until 1942 at the earliest, the Treaty gave Hitler complete freedom of action. Nevertheless he repeatedly reassured Mussolini that he, too, agreed that the Axis needed three more years of peace before embarking on war.

ITALIAN NEUTRALITY, SEPTEMBER 1939–JUNE 1940

By August, it was clear that Hitler was preparing for what he hoped would be a localised war against Poland. The decision for war took the Italians by surprise and for two weeks Mussolini could not make up his mind whether or not to join Hitler. For a dictator who had constantly described war as the school of the nation and predicted a victorious struggle against the decadent democracies, it was humiliating to remain neutral, but in the end on 20 August he was convinced by Ciano that the Germans had broken their pledge not to go to war for three years. Even more importantly, Mussolini realised that the Italian armed forces were simply not ready for war. His only way out of the Pact was to tell Hitler that the Italians would fight if the Germans gave them the necessary equipment. When Hitler asked him what he needed, the list drawn up on 26 August was so long that it was obvious that Italians were seeking an excuse to remain neutral.

On 29 August Mussolini made an abortive effort to repeat his success at Munich by proposing another four-power conference to be held on 5 September to find a solution to the Polish problem, but this was firmly rejected by Hitler, who proceeded to attack Poland on 1 September. Britain and France then declared war on Germany two days later and Italy remained neutral. Mussolini was uncomfortably aware of the parallel with Italy's neutrality in 1914, which he had then so scornfully attacked. He had three realistic options: he could at the right moment intervene on the German side, he could remain neutral, or he could create a third force of neutral countries under Italian leadership. The Allies hoped that Italy, as in 1915, could even be persuaded to join them, but Mussolini consistently rebuffed their advances. He did for a short period consider creating a neutral bloc consisting of Spain and the Balkan countries, but this idea was soon dropped. Ciano informed the German Ambassador on 17 October that

> In no circumstances did the Duce want to be made the spokesman
> of the neutrals. He simply detested the word because Italy

belonged neither to the belligerents nor to the neutrals; her status as before remained that of maximum preparedness for which the *Duce* was working by every means in order to be ready at any given moment.

(Quoted in *Italian Foreign Policy*, p. 356)

ITALY ENTERS THE WAR

When Mussolini met Hitler on the Brenner on 18 March 1940, he informed him that 'Italy's entry into the war [was] inevitable'. He was helped to this conclusion by Hitler's absolute confidence in victory and veiled warnings that Italy would get nothing of the spoils unless she came off the fence. In the end it was the string of German victories, starting with the occupation of Norway in April and ending with the defeat of France in June, that persuaded Mussolini finally to intervene on 10 June. He wanted above all to benefit from the great redistribution of territory and colonies that was expected to follow the defeat of France and Britain. Like his predecessors in 1915 he assumed that the war would soon be over, but unlike them he took Italy in on the side that was eventually to lose.

timeline	1936	July	Spanish Civil War starts
		October	Rome–Berlin Axis
	1937	December	Italy withdraws from the League of Nations
	1938	March	The *Anschluss*
		September	The Munich Crisis
	1939	April	Italian occupation of Albania
		May	Pact of Steel
		September	Britain and France declare war on Germany
	1940	June	Italy declares war on Britain and France

Points to consider

1) **Did Mussolini continue to pursue in the years 1936–40 the traditional Italian policy of balancing between Germany, Britain and France?**
2) **Why did Mussolini accept the *Anschluss* so tamely in March 1938?**

3) Why did Mussolini wait until June 1940 before declaring war on Britain and France?

4) To what extent did Mussolini still regard Germany as a threat during the period July 1936–June 1940?

10

MILITARY DEFEAT AND THE DOWNFALL OF MUSSOLINI

A RECORD OF FAILURE, 1940–3

It was ironic that Mussolini who had made the glorification of war one of the main themes of Fascism was to lead Italy into the worst and most humiliating defeat in her history. In June 1940 he intended to fight a 'parallel war' alongside Germany to gain control of the Mediterranean and the surrounding territories. Convinced that the Axis powers were invincible he also had a vision of a grand Fascist 'New Order' in Europe which was to be constructed by Italy and Germany. After the fall of France in June 1940 he had initially hoped that this would be achieved with very little real fighting, but Britain's determination to fight, and Hitler's postponement of his plan for an invasion of England, meant that Italy would have to take the offensive. An initial and fatal mistake made by Mussolini was not to concentrate on one campaign at a time, which might well have brought him some success. Instead he launched two campaigns in the autumn of 1940, one against Greece and the other against the British in Egypt. The war against Greece was as much aimed against Hitler as the British since Mussolini wished to counter German influence in the Balkans, particularly Romania. In both theatres the parallel and independent war came to an abrupt end. In Egypt in December 1940 General Graziani's forces were pushed back into Libya with the loss of 380 tanks and 130 000 prisoners taken, and by May 1941 British Commonwealth forces advancing from Kenya had occupied the whole of the Italian East African Empire, including Ethiopia. In the Balkans the Greeks not only defeated the Italians but advanced into Albania. In both North Africa and the Balkans the Germans had to intervene and from that point on the Italians inevitably became junior partners in a German war rather than fighting their own parallel war. In the Balkans they were initially given by the Germans control of Dalmatia, most of Slovenia, Croatia and Montenegro, but Mussolini's brutally repressive policy led to a bitter guerrilla war which tied down half a million Italian troops. In North Africa the Germans steadied the front in 1941, but by October 1942 they too were in retreat and in May 1943 all the Axis forces in North Africa surrendered to British, Commonwealth and American forces.

Although Mussolini resented being a junior partner to the Germans and occasionally through Swiss intermediaries made tentative approaches to the British about the possibilities of a separate peace, he realised that the best chance for the survival of Fascism was a German victory. In 1941, still convinced that Hitler would win the war, he insisted on sending 227 000 ill-equipped troops to the Russian front to ensure that when the peace conference came Hitler would not treat Italy as if it were Spain or Vichy France.

Mussolini's fate was sealed when Churchill managed to persuade the Americans that Italy should be invaded from North Africa. Churchill believed that Italy was the 'soft underbelly of Europe' and that Allied troops would quickly be able to advance up to the Alps and overthrow the Fascist regime. Allied troops landed in Sicily on 9 July and 16 days later Mussolini was indeed overthrown, but that was not to lead to peace as the Germans occupied Italy and forced the Allies to fight their way up the peninsula.

Mussolini as war leader

Despite Mussolini's frequent boasting that he could mobilise an army of 'eight million bayonets' and an airforce that could 'blot out the sun', he had done little to modernise the armed forces before the war. Anxious to keep the support of the admirals and the officer corps, who wanted, like most officers at the time, simply to turn the clock back to 1913, he had given them a free hand. Thus, despite some excellent ideas from a few enterprising officers, in 1939 the Italian armed forces were not in a position to fight a modern war. Furthermore the losses in equipment suffered in Ethiopia and especially Spain had not been made good.

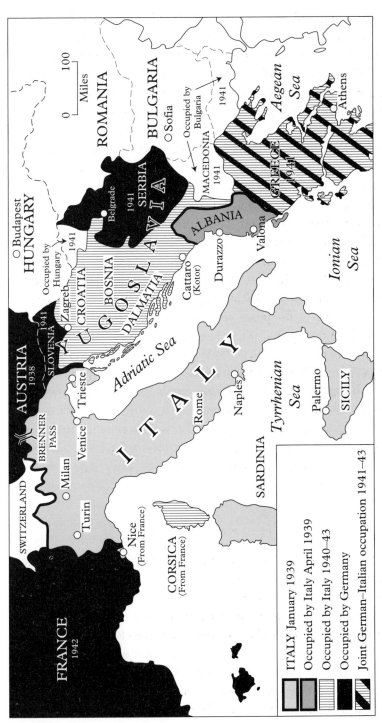

Italian expansion in Europe, 1939–43

SWITZERLAND

AUSTRIA
1938

FRANCE
1942

BRENNER
PASS

SLOVENIA
1941

HUNGARY
○ Budapest

Occupied by
Hungary
1941

ROMANIA

BULGARIA

○ Sofia

Occupied by
Bulgaria
1941

MACEDONIA
1941

Aegean
Sea

○ Athens

GREECE
1941

SERBIA

Belgrade
1941

ALBANIA

Valona ○

Durazzo ○

Cattaro
(Kotor) ○

Zagreb ○

CROATIA

BOSNIA

DALMATIA

Y U G O S L A V I A

Adriatic Sea

Ionian
Sea

Trieste ○

Venice ○

Milan ○

Turin ○

Nice
(From France) ○

Rome □

Naples ○

Palermo ○

SICILY

I T A L Y

Tyrrhenian
Sea

SARDINIA

CORSICA
(From France)

100
Miles
0

ITALY January 1939
Occupied by Italy April 1939
Occupied by Italy 1940–43
Occupied by Germany
Joint German–Italian occupation 1941–43

99

Mussolini stifled any debate and ensured that his propaganda services gave an entirely misleading picture of the situation.

He also failed to build up an efficient military and civil staff which would have enabled him to delegate work to subordinates, but then delegating was not something that Mussolini liked doing. The whole Fascist structure in Italy was dependent on the myth that the *Duce* never made a mistake and that his pronouncements were always right. Not surprisingly Mussolini was unable to master the enormous volume of business that flowed into his office. His chief of police observed that by 'trying to control everything he was deceived and disobeyed by almost everyone'. He was, too, an ageing and very sick man, with frequent and crippling stomach pains possibly caused by a peptic ulcer, who had to spend long periods away from Rome on his country estate.

THE ECONOMY AND THE HOME FRONT

Once Italy entered the war, her supply problems became acute and contributed greatly to her eventual defeat. She could only import 1.5 million tonnes of oil from Romania, which was more than 50 per cent below her peacetime consumption. Similarly she was dependent on German coal, of which she received only just under a million tonnes a month. It was small wonder then that her steel production fell from 2.3 million tonnes in 1938 to 1.9 million tonnes in 1942. The whole economy suffered from shortages. There was hardly any fuel in the northern cities in the winter of 1942–3, shoe leather ran out and soap and coffee were unobtainable luxuries. Rationing was introduced at the barely adequate level of 1000 calories a day. Food production also fell as peasants were called up into the army and artificial fertilisers and animal feeds could no longer be imported. In northern Italy production was hit further by the bombing of the industrial cities. Production was seriously disrupted, workers' flats were destroyed and thousands fled from the cities.

The Fascist Party, as in the years of the Depression, was organised to assist the people in the far greater emergency of the war. It was responsible for civil defence, and the welfare of both combatants and their families as well as evacuees from the towns. It was also supposed to supervise the requisitioning of and control of prices of foodstuffs and basic consumer goods. Its failure to do this effectively increased its unpopularity. Similarly its primary role of defending Mussolini and the Fascist regime was made more difficult by the long catalogue of Italian military defeats.

Mussolini also began to make enemies of the middle classes who had supported him in 1922 by increasing taxation and failing to control inflation, and he alarmed the officer corps by proposing to create a new classless army. Tactlessly but all too accurately he announced in April 1942 that 'we always said we despised the comfortable life, and now the uncomfortable life has arrived'.

THE GROWTH OF OPPOSITION

By the early summer of 1943 opposition to Fascist rule was growing throughout Italy. In March 1943 over 100 000 workers in Turin went on strike and similar protests flared up in Piedmont and Lombardy. Anti-Fascist groups were also beginning to emerge. The remnants of the pre-Fascist Republicans, Radicals and Left Liberals set up a 'Party of Action' in January 1943, the Communists and Socialists began to rebuild their local organisations and the Catholics formed a new Christian Democratic Party. All these, however, were still too weak to overthrow Mussolini. For that the King, the army and opposition within the Fascist Party itself was needed.

MUSSOLINI'S OVERTHROW

Mussolini unwisely created a powerful dissident group within the Party when in February 1943 he sacked half his Cabinet, amongst whom were the key figures of Grandi, Ciano and Bottai. Their desire for revenge was strengthened by the almost daily evidence that Italy had lost the war. It was known that the Allies would not negotiate with Mussolini, but unofficial contacts with the Americans through the Papacy indicated that Washington would be ready to negotiate with an Italian military government chosen by the King. Once the Allies invaded Sicily, it was obvious that the war was lost and that Mussolini would have to be deposed. The bombing of Rome for two hours on 19 July merely reinforced that message.

On 24–25 July 1943 the Grand Council met for a marathon ten-hour session and at its conclusion voted by 19 votes to 7 to ask the King to resume command of the armed forces and 'that supreme initiative of decision making which our institutions attribute to him'. This was in fact a request for him to replace Mussolini. Throughout the proceedings Mussolini was so apathetic and ineffectual that one of his biographers, Mack Smith, has speculated that he was 'consciously or unconsciously . . . seeking a pretext to disengage honourably from Berlin, or even perhaps to abdicate and leave someone else to take the decisions he did not know how to or dared not take'. The following day Mussolini began to have second thoughts and to talk about punishing the 'traitors', but when he visited the King that afternoon, he was told that Marshal Badoglio, the former Chief of Staff, would take over, and he was arrested on leaving the palace. He was first sent to the penal settlement on the island of Ponza and then later moved to an isolated skiing resort from where he was rescued by German commandos on 12 September and taken to Germany.

THE REPUBLIC OF SALÒ

On 3 September 1943 General Castellano, Badoglio's envoy in Lisbon, negotiated a secret cease-fire with the Allies. British Commonwealth and American troops then landed on the mainland of Italy. The Germans responded by occupying Rome and the King and Badoglio had to flee southwards to the protection of the Allies. Mussolini was restored by Hitler as the head of a Fascist regime, the so-called Italian Social Republic in central and northern Italy, which was in reality a German puppet state. It soon became known as the 'Republic of Salò', after its Ministry of Popular Culture and Propaganda, which had its offices in the small town of Salò. The Germans treated northern Italy as if it were occupied territory. Italian soldiers were interned in Germany and used as cheap labour in factories, Italian machinery and sometimes whole industrial plants were also moved there and young men were called up like their contemporaries in France and elsewhere for industrial service in the *Reich*.

Mussolini made some effort to relaunch Fascism. He accused the King, the conservative bourgeoisie and above all those who had voted against him on the Grand Council on 24–25 July of having prevented the Fascist revolution from taking place over the last 20 years. He proclaimed that Fascism would now 'return to its origins' and the ideas of 1915–19. The programme of the new Republican Fascist Party was announced at the Verona Congress in November 1943. It was a rehash of old ideas, except that it promised to call an assembly and draw up a constitution with an elected head of state. Corporatism was to be replaced by a form of 'socialisation'. All large firms were to be run by boards on which 50 per cent of the members would be elected by the workers and the state itself would run the basic industries. Many of the arguments of the early 1920s re-emerged. Was for instance Party membership to be confined to a dynamic élite or was the Party to consist of a mass membership?

Hostilities dragged on for another 18 months as the Allies slowly advanced up the peninsula. In the Salò Republic a bitter civil war broke out. In September 1943 groups of Italian soldiers and urban evacuees took to the hills and became partisans. They were subsequently reinforced by large numbers of young men who fled rather than be deported to Germany. They became experts in guerrilla warfare, and by June 1944 Mussolini only controlled the plain bordering both banks of the river Po.

In April 1945 the Allies at last reached Bologna. Mussolini meanwhile attempted in turn to negotiate with the Allies and the partisans. He also thought of escape to Spain or even Argentina, but he had left it too late. In the end he joined a group of German soldiers who were trying to get through the partisan lines to Austria. Despite trying to disguise himself in a German greatcoat and helmet he was recognised, seized by the partisans and shot. His body, together with those of several other leading Fascists and his mistress, was thrown onto a lorry, driven to Milan and hung upside down at the filling station in Piazzale Loreto where in August 1944 15 Italian hostages had been executed by the Fascists.

| _timeline_ | 1941 | | Italians defeated in Greece and North Africa |
| | 1943 | March | Strikes in Turin |

	July	Allied landings in Sicily
		Mussolini's fall from power
	September	Salò Republic set up
1944	June	Rome occupied by Allies
1945	April	Mussolini shot by partisans

Points to consider

1) Was Mussolini alone responsible for Italy's disastrous defeat in the Second World War?
2) Was Mussolini's fall in July 1943 caused primarily by military defeat?
3) Was the Salò Republic ever anything more than a German puppet state?

11

MUSSOLINI'S SIGNIFICANCE AND HIS LEGACY

In reaction to defeat in war, occupation and the bitter partisan conflict in the north, Italians were reluctant until the 1960s to begin the difficult and painful task of reassessing Mussolini and the Fascist era and of placing them within the context of their history. The ideals and the record of the Resistance were regarded as virtually sacred and as late as the mid-1970s it was still a criminal offence to criticise them. Given the crimes and brutalities of Fascism this was an understandable reaction, but it did inhibit research into what Fascism really was. Gradually with the increasing availability of more documentary evidence and the emergence of a younger generation of historians, it became easier to assess more rationally not only the crimes and failures of Fascism but also its political successes.

It is easy to paint Mussolini as a brutal buffoon, who kept changing his mind, and to forget that he was a formidable politician, even though he profited enormously from the weaknesses of his opponents. In 1944 he remarked to the new Party Secretary, Pavolini, that 'Fascism is Mussolinism . . . What would Fascism be if I had not been.' Mussolini did not create Fascism as such. The *Fascio di Conbattimento* which he formed in Milan in March 1919 was a small, obscure group that had little impact on national politics. The real birth of Fascism as a political force occurred when spontaneously local *fasci* or bands under their own leaders set themselves up throughout rural Italy between the autumn and spring of 1920 and 1921. Mussolini's skill was to project their demands nationally through his paper *Il Popola d'Italia* and to turn them into a political force. In considering Mussolini's exploitation of the prolonged political crisis of the autumn of 1922 it is hard not to agree with one of his biographers, Ivan Kirkpatrick, that 'his patience, his judgement and his timing could not have been bettered'.

Once Prime Minister he was skilfully able to tame the revolutionary wing of the Fascist Party and consolidate his position by allying with the Conservatives, the industrialists and the traditional forces of the state such as the army and the civil service. By 1929 Mussolini had created in de Felice's phrase a 'regime', which in the final analysis rested on a consensus of support amongst the Italian people for himself. In the long term, however, the prospects of the regime surviving his death were slight as it did not develop a new ruling class and was dependent on his charisma for the continuing support it gained in Italy.

Initially Fascism was a revolutionary movement, but inevitably the compromises it concluded with the Conservatives turned it to a great extent into a counter-revolutionary force. The American historian, E. R. Tannenbaum, for instance argued that 'more than anything else the labor policies of the Fascist regime made its claims to being revolutionary a mockery'. Yet it did not become just another reactionary force; its revolutionary potential never quite vanished. Mussolini had established the first Fascist regime in Europe and he managed through the Party during the Depression and the Ethiopian war politically to mobilise the Italian masses and to win their support or at least their consent to his rule.

In most ways the legacy of Fascism was negative and destructive: a lost war, a country turned into a battlefield on which a protracted struggle between the Allies and the Germans was waged, and a harsh peace treaty signed in Paris in 1947. By this Italy lost all her empire except Somalia. Dalmatia, Istria and Fiume were handed back to Yugoslavia and she had to pay reparations to Greece, Yugoslavia and the USSR. However in certain defined financial and economic areas the legacy of Fascism was more positive. The IRI and the state-owned oil corporation, AGIP, for instance, played an important part in the Italian economic miracle of the 1950s. Unlike Nazism, which was theroetically an anti-modernist movement although it ended up accelerating the industrialisation of Germany, Fascism was not hostile to technical and economic change. But it wanted modernity without any of the political and social consequences, such as democracy and pluralism, which went hand in hand with modernisation in Britain, France and America. Only in his attempts to keep women in the home and the peasants in the countryside did Mussolini try to put the clock back.

The Lateran Accords, which had brought to an end 50 years of hostility between the Papacy and the Italians, remained in place after the collapse of Fascism and the new Catholic Christian Democratic Party became a major political force in Italy. After 1945 the Fascist Party was outlawed, but there were successor groups such as the Everyman Party and the Italian Social Movement, which in 1994 won 100 seats and joined Silvio Berlusconi's coalition. Arguably Fascism's most lasting legacy was that the Italian people learnt from its failures. As Martin Clark observed 'Post-Fascist Italy was set up as the regime's inverted image: a peace loving, democratic, de-centralized republic, guaranteeing civil liberties and run by men with impeccable anti-Fascist credentials'.

Points to consider

1) What if anything did Mussolini achieve?
2) Did Mussolini modernise Italy?
3) Did the Italian people support Mussolini for most of the time?
4) 'Absurd buffoon' or a 'wily politician.' Which assessment of Mussolini is nearer to the truth?

12

HISTORIOGRAPHY AND BIBLIOGRAPHY

ITALIAN HISTORIOGRAPHY, 1925–45

Italian books on Mussolini and Fascism during this period divide into two sharply opposing camps: the Fascist and the anti-Fascist which for the most part were written abroad by political exiles. The books produced by Fascists and 'fellow travellers' were inevitably sycophantic and interesting more as examples of propaganda than historiography. For instance in 1926 Mussolini's mistress wrote a glowing account of her lover's many political, cultural and military skills. Later when she was dropped by Mussolini, she admitted that the book was totally inaccurate because 'invention was more useful than truth'. In theory Mussolini wrote his own official autobiography, *My Biography* (published in London by Hutchinson in 1928), but in fact it was ghosted by his brother and the former American ambassador, Richard Washburn Child.

For more critical assessments the historian has to look to the books written by Italian exiles and refugees. In welcome contrast to the propaganda described above they seek to explain how Mussolini seized power and to analyse the regime he created. One of the most informative studies of this type is A. Rossi's (pseudonym for A. Taxa) *The Rise of Italian Fascism* published by Methuen in 1938. Rossi concentrated on the mistakes made by the Socialists and showed how skilfully Mussolini exaggerated the threat from the Left to establish his dictatorship. He pointed out that 'much of his strength has come from the weakness of his enemies. In 1919 he was simultaneously outbidding the demagogues and working for the cause of reaction.' By far the most well-known of the Italian exiles was Gaetano Salvemini, the former

Professor of History at Florence University, who was forced into exile in 1925. His three books written between 1927 and 1936 have been described by Roberto Vivarelli as 'milestones in the literature on Italian Fascism' and show how the Liberals, the army, the Crown and the Catholic Church tolerated the creation of a Fascist dictatorship. In *Under the Axe of Fascism*, Gollancz, 1936, Salvemini subjected the Italian corporate state to a devastating analysis. In one unforgettable chapter title he compares trying to find out what the corporations really did to 'looking in a dark room for a black cat which is not there'.

Another group of contemporary Italian historians, most of whom were members of the Liberal Democratic Movement, adopted a line of interpretation called the 'revelation thesis' in which Mussolini's success was essentially attributed to the backward nature of Italian politics.

BRITISH AND AMERICAN HISTORIOGRAPHY, 1922–45

In the 1920s British historians were unclear how to interpret Mussolini's success. G. M. Trevelyan, like those adopting the 'revelation thesis', saw 'the historical cause of the present state of affairs in Italy as residing in the unbroken millennial continuity of the politics of the piazza'. In the 1930s as the Nazi threat began to overshadow Europe, left-wing historians, particularly, began to look more carefully at the history of Fascist Italy. Of course a large number of these books were little more than current affairs, but arguably the two best studies are H. Finer, *Mussolini's Italy*, Gollancz, 1935, and G. Megaro, *Mussolini in the Making*, Allen and Unwin, 1938. The latter author, an American historian, devoted most of his book to exposing the Mussolini legend by careful but sometimes dangerous research in Italy itself, while Finer produced a very useful analysis of the institutions of the Fascist state.

PROBLEMS FACING ITALIAN HISTORIANS

Until the 1960s most Italian historians steered clear of Fascism as it was still a too recent and painful experience. Any studies that did appear were straightforward narrative accounts. Marxists saw Fascism as the weapon used by an anti-democratic ruling class to control the workers, while Liberals, in Bernedetto Croce's words, dismissed it as 'an intellectual and moral disease' which affected Italy at a time of crisis. Essentially they felt that Fascism could not be studied like other movements of the time such as Liberalism, Socialism and democracy. It was an irrational barbarism best confined to oblivion.

TWO BRITISH BIOGRAPHICAL STUDIES

In 1962 Christopher Hibbert's *Benito Mussolini* was published by Longman. It is an interesting but essentially narrative study which gives the reader a well-written and colourful account of Mussolini. The key years of 1920–2 are, however, rather perfunctorily dealt with, although he gives a good account of foreign affairs and of Mussolini's downfall. A fuller and more analytical account was written in 1964 by the former British diplomat Ivan Kirkpatrick. *Mussolini. A Study of a Demagogue* (Odhams). Although his account of Italian foreign and domestic policy is necessarily limited by lack of access to the relevant archival material, his overall assessment of Mussolini's place in history is interesting and anticipates some of the revisionist ideas of the younger historians:

> His end obscured his achievements, which were considerable. His place in history is assured if only because he was the first man to launch a new form of Socialism, the Socialism of Nationalism.

> (p. 188)

DE FELICE AND THE REVISIONIST HISTORIOGRAPHY

Meanwhile the younger generation. of Italian historians was at last beginning to get to grips with the phenomenon of Fascism. Their painful probing and efforts to put Fascism within the context of Italian history met with both shock and anger in Italy. Not surprisingly one historian, P. Ungari, observed that whenever 'one shows signs of shifting away slightly from the strait-jacket of Fascism as pure historical negativity (freedom crushed by authoritarianism, irrational barbarism and violent class domination), one immediately senses the charges of an offence against anti-Fascism' (quoted in the *Journal of Contemporary*

History, **21**, 1986, p. 181). Undeterred by this the Italian scholar Renzo De Felice, in a series of articles, books, and above all in his multi-volume but unfinished biography of Mussolini (seven volumes of which appeared between 1965 and 1990, published by Einaudi, Turin), proceeded to analyse Fascism. He came to the conclusion that the Fascist movement was composed essentially of an 'emerging middle class' which wanted political power. Unlike Nazism it was a modernising force which, as he controversially described it, was 'vital', 'optimistic' and 'creative', and by the mid 1930s had forged a consensus which enjoyed the support of most Italians. De Felice concedes that once Mussolini seized power he had to compromise with the Establishment and that a difference then developed between a relatively conservative Fascist regime and the still revolutionary 'Fascism movement', which was composed of people who joined the party in order to bring about radical change in Italy. He argues that this 'movement' was essentially a revolutionary force of the left, and, although it was suppressed, it potentially remained a threat to conservative interests right up to 1943. De Felice thus forced not only his fellow Italians but also other European and American historians to take a new look at Fascism. De Felice himself became a controversial figure who was seen by many to be erecting, in Mack Smith's words, 'a monument to the *Duce*'. The gist of his ideas can be found in *Interpretations of Fascism*, ed. B. H. Everett, Cambridge, Massachusetts/London, 1977. There are also several review articles of his work, the best of which is by B. W. Painter: 'Renzo de Felice and the Historiography of Italian Fascism' in the *American Historical Review*, **95**(2), 1990.

Thanks largely to De Felice, who has rightly been called the father of Italian revisionism, there has been an enormous increase in work on Italian Fascism. As listing the books and articles published would take some 50 pages, only a small number of easily accessible British and American titles can be mentioned.

General works

A well-written and concise account of Fascist Italy is contained in M. Clark's *Modern Italy, 1871–1982* (Longman, 1985). More detailed studies of the Fascist era, which also take note of recent research, have been written by E. Tannenbaum, *Fascism in Italy, Society and Culture*,

1922–45 (Allen Lane, 1973), De Grand, *Italian Fascism. Its Origins and Development* (2nd edition) (University of Nebraska Press, 1994), P. Morgan, *Italian Fascism, 1919–1945* (Macmillan, 1995), and J. Whittam, *Fascist Italy* (Manchester University Press, 1995). M. Blinkhorn's *Mussolini and Fascist Italy* (Lancaster Pamphlets, 1994) is an excellent but very brief survey of the period.

Specialised works

Fascism's links with business and industry are covered by R. Sarti, *Fascism and the Industrial Leadership in Italy* (University of California Press, 1971). The best study of the background to the signature of the Lateran Pacts is in J. F. Pollard, *The Vatican and Italian Fascism, 1929–32* (Cambridge University Press, 1985). An interesting study of the Fascist regime's attempt to control the population is in D. Thompson, *State Control in Fascist Italy. Culture and Conformity, 1925–43* (Manchester University Press, 1991). Denis Mack Smith has written a readable and very well researched biography of *Mussolini* (Weidenfeld and Nicolson, 1981; reprinted as a Phoenix Paperback in 1994), which is also refreshingly free of jargon and sceptical of some of the revisionists' conclusions.

HISTORIOGRAPHY OF ITALIAN FOREIGN POLICY

As with Mussolini's domestic policy, works on his foreign policy in the years immediately after 1945 were dominated by a revulsion against the cruelties and inefficiencies of Fascism. In Italy Salvemini again led the way in the second edition of his *Mussolino Diplomatico* (Bari, 1952), in which he not only condemned Mussolini's diplomacy, but argued that it was improvised virtually on a daily basis for propaganda purposes. Nobody convincingly refuted this in the 1940s or 1950s. Elizabeth Wiskemann, for instance, in the classic account of Mussolini's relations with Hitler, *The Rome–Berlin Axis* (Oxford University Press, 1949; reprinted by Fontana in 1966), argued that he had no clear aims at all and 'for many years . . . had rolled his eyes and brandished his chin, as he shouted cruel phrases with Romagnal violence'. As the Italian government began to publish the diplomatic documents covering the

Fascist period, historians were able to take a more informed view of Mussolini's foreign policy. By the end of the 1960s the new Italian revisionist school had re-interpreted much of Mussolini's foreign policy. Most historians came to agree with Ennio Di Nolfo, Professor of History at the University of Florence, that Mussolini had a 'clear and early awareness of his objectives' even though he viewed the Italian Foreign Office 'as a branch of the Ministry of Propaganda'.

Clark, Morgan, Whittam and Le Grand all have useful and up-to-date chapters on Mussolini's foreign policy. C. J. Lowe and F. Marzari, *Italian Foreign Policy, 1870–1940* (Routledge, 1975), is indispensable for Franco–Italian relations, Mussolini's Balkans policy and the period September 1939–June 1940. R. J. B. Bosworth in *Italy, the Least of the Great Powers: Italian Foreign Policy Before the First World War* (Cambridge University Press, 1980), argues that what was different about the foreign policy of Liberal as compared with Fascist Italy was not the aims but the methods. Mussolini's initial foreign policy is covered by A. Cassels, *Mussolini's Early Diplomacy* (Princeton University Press, 1970). He stresses that Mussolini's aggressive intentions did exist in the 1920s but that the professional diplomats at the Foreign Office were able to a great extent to control them.

There are a large number of books on Italian imperial and foreign policy in the 1930s. Particularly important studies are by Esmonde Robertson, *Mussolini as Empire-Builder: Europe and Africa, 1932–36* (Macmillan, 1977) and D. Mack Smith, *Mussolini's Roman Empire* (Penguin, 1976). The two writers diasagree profoundly over the motivations behind Mussolini's foreign policy. Robertson sees Mussolini's policy as being determined by his desire to control strategic points in the Mediterranean, whereas Mack Smith again sees Mussolini as a wordy showman with no rational policy. Italian intervention in Spain is covered by J. Coverdale, *Italian Intervention in the Spanish Civil War* (Princeton University Press, 1975), who stresses that Mussolini was primarily interested in securing Italy's position in the western Mediterranean. For the Axis Agreement and Italy's growing links with Germany after 1936 leading up to the declaration of war in June 1940 D. C. Watt's short article, 'The Rome–Berlin Axis: 1936–1940 (*Review of Politics*, XXII (October 1960) is an important classic, arguing that it was signed mainly for propaganda reasons. De Felice's assessment of Mussolini's early foreign policy does not significantly differ from the other revisionist historians. He believed that he had specific aims, although initially 'it was essentially a function of Mussolini's domestic policy'. After the Ethiopian War his views become more controversial when he argues that despite the Axis and even the Pact of Steel Mussolini still wanted to balance between Britain and Germany. M. Knox's *Mussolini Unleashed, 1939–1941: Politics and Strategy in Fascist Italy's Last War* (Cambridge University Press, 1986), is a detailed examination of Mussolini's war aims. Still the best study of Mussolini's fall and his relations with the Germans during the Salò Republic is F. W. Deakin, *The Brutal Friendship. Mussolini, Hitler and the Fall of Italian Fascism* (Weidenfeld and Nicolson, 1962).

FASCISM AND NAZISM: COMPARATIVE STUDIES

Following E. Nolte's pioneering *Three Faces of Fascism* (Munich, Piper, 1963), historians have paid considerable attention to the European context of Italian Fascism and its relation to Nazism. Nolte himself and many other historians argue that the two movements are similar in aims and origins and can both be described as 'Fascist'. There are, however, many who disagree. Sarti and Tannenbaum, for instance, argue that Italian Fascism, unlike Nazism was a modernising force, while De Felice stresses that Mussolini's foreign policy was essentially imperialist in the old nineteenth-century tradition. The German historian Hildebrand, in *The Third Reich* (reprinted by Routledge, 1991), interestingly observes that 'Mussolini still thought in familiar historical categories, whereas Hitler's ideas burst the bounds of tradition: they were intended to precipitate the course of History and finally bring it to a standstill in a biological utopia.' (p. 118). Yet when one considers Mussolini's introduction of anti-semitic measures in Italy, of his attempts to liquidate Ethiopian intellectuals and of his plans for 'living space' in Albania, it may be that the difference between the policies of the two dictators, at any rate in their racial and foreign policies, is one of scale rather than of kind.

Points to consider

1) **What were the difficulties for historians writing about the Fascist regime during the period 1922–1960?**

2) Why did the work of the revisionist historians in the 1960s and 1970s cause so much controversy in Italy and elsewhere?

3) Do you agree with Hildebrand that Mussolini 'still thought in familiar historical categories'?

INDEX